On To The
Prize

By
Renee Hibma

Vision of Hope Publishing
Lakeland, Florida

Copyright © 2015 Renee Hibma

Published by:
VISION OF HOPE PUBLISHING
Lakeland, Florida, U.S.A.

All rights reserved. No part of this book may be reproduced or transmitted in any form or by any means, electronic or mechanical, including photocopying, recording, or by any information storage and retrieval system, without written permission from the author, except for the inclusion of brief quotations in a review. For information, contact the publisher at revdrrenee@juno.com.

All emphasis with capital letters relating to God and pronouns referring to God are the author's choice.

Paperback ISBN 978-1-329-05159-1
E-book ISBN 978-1-311-18650-8

Cover design: Rick Hoover
Inside illustrations: Melanie Hoover

Editors: Elva Hoover and Susan Parsons Sumner

Scripture taken from the King James Version.
Scripture "modernized" at author's discretion.

Printed in the United States of America.

CONTENTS

FOREWORD	vii
ACKNOWLEDGMENTS	x
PREFACE	xii
INTRODUCTION: The Race	xiii

CHAPTERS

The Pottery	1
Flight Feathers	5
Are We Skating By?	11
Communicating Is Such a Sacrifice!	16
Den of Thieves	22
How Vital Are You in the Kingdom of God?	25
Who Guards the Shepherd?	28
Pain	34
Remember Noah	37
Winter	40
Fruit	43
Roots	47
What Are You Listening to?	54
The Shed	58
Clouds	61
Black Top	65
Tastefulness	69
Lovesick	72
How's Your Salt Level?	78
A Pressure Washer	85
A Plantin--g of the Lord	88
Applying God's Word	93
Flavor	95
Progression to Destruction	98
Gravitational Pull	104
Hearing God	107
Hard Lesson	111
Leadership	115

Disconnected	118
Mountains	120
A Subtle Sin	122
The Lion of Judah	124
Lukewarm	127
Road Signs	129
Servanthood	132
Difficult Relationships	134
Warfare	137
Wisdom	139
Jonah	143
Trust	147
A Child	151
Relay Race	153
Leah or Rachael?	154
ABOUT THE AUTHOR	162

Dedicated to

Gary and Gloria Hibma
Bob and Kaye Garrison
and
Lewis and Doris Smith

My mom went to be with Jesus this year. She didn't get to read my book. My dad went twenty-three years ago. Together, they instilled principles in my life – that enable me not only to survive in this world, but to thrive through obedience to Christ. Those principles were rooted in Jesus, and found a heritage of expression through music.

Both of the other couples were fathers and mothers in the faith to me. Without their love and guidance and prayer, I never would have made it this far with my sanity—or my life, for that matter! God knows just who we need in our lives just when we need them. I am thankful for these godly influences.

To Mom and Dad, Bob, Kaye, and Doris, who are with Jesus now, enjoying the full presence of God: I love all of you so much and cannot give enough praise to our Father
for having put you in my life!

FOREWORD

If you are reading this book, you are probably a Christian. And you're probably running hard on the track, reaching out your hands for that bottle of water in the middle of the race to the finish line. This book is one of those bottles. It's a refreshing dose of encouragement for tired and thirsty runners. And it's written in an easy, friendly, conversational style—as if you're sharing a cappuccino and a Krispy Kreme doughnut with your best friend.

Renee Hibma is an encourager, an exhorter—a coach. And she is able to "...comfort them which are in any trouble, by the comfort wherewith we ourselves are comforted of God" (I Corinthians 1:4). She gets this ability by the Spirit—it's the result of a life laid down in death to self. That kind of crucified life results in a subsequent resurrection—and not just in the hereafter. It renders a new view of life's present circumstances, a way of seeing things so that we grow by it in knowledge and character and trust in God. It's a playing out of Romans 5: "...tribulation worketh patience; And patience, [results in] experience; and experience, [results in] hope..."

And that resultant hope is a new approach to all of life. It is the love of God—a new love FOR God—because we know He's faithful to bring things around for our good. This love is shed abroad in our hearts by the Holy Ghost which is given unto us when we receive it! We have to LET patience have her perfect work, that we may be perfect and entire. (James 1:4) This is what Renee has done, and she submits the same opportunity to her readers.

I've known Renee since we were 13. We went to the same church. We were both gifted musicians, able to pick out vocal harmonies on virtually any song; playing piano by ear...We were really unusual kids, I guess! Our unpopular faith caused us to endure some hardness at school, having been baptized by fire during the "Jesus Movement" revival days, and having forsaken all for the sake of the call; taking our Bibles to school, organizing and attending early morning Bible studies. We found refuge in friends of like mind, and in music.

But the years following our high school graduation would prove us. Music and friendships were not enough, because God was exacting greater things of us. He taught us that nothing satisfies if you're still viewing the world by the world. Even music—Christian music—can feed the flesh; and Christian friendships can usurp the Lordship of Jesus in decision-making, devotion.

In the confusing world mix of secularism, religion, truth, tradition, temptation and ego, we would find ourselves weighed, but wanting. Over several decades, she and I both learned that the anchor of our souls was not a church, or a gifting, music, or even Christian friends. It was rather the person of Jesus! It took afflictions, persecutions, temptations and adversities to prove our mettle—to try our faith; to pursue our own designs or to pursue the Will of God; to learn to forsake ambition and let God lead. We lived a thousand miles apart, yet both of us were in the same crucible of life, designed to reveal our respective lack, and spur us on a quest for deeper truth. We have both overcome the allure of this world with our faith intact. The empowerment that has emerged from those victories is a way of seeing ordinary things from a spiritual perspective. Renee sees life in this way, and shares these nuggets of wisdom beautifully in this refreshing, unpretentious and practical book.

On To The Prize will help take you to the finish! It's a compilation of life-lessons rooted in simple observations—things you've seen yourself, like bird wings and broken vases, pressure washers and roadsigns. Out of each observation comes unexpected insight to help the reader learn to think differently—it's not the stuff of this world; it's a spiritual perspective.

This almost reads like a devotional book, but the chapters run longer and deeper. Safely interwoven with relevant Scriptural references, this book has a solid foundation, and Renee's personal experiences and insights are well worth sharing. In fact, this book would make a terrific tool for group Bible study and discussion or personal reading.

As you read this book, receive it as a modern epistle from one of the most personable women in ministry today. I know that her heart is set toward empowering the runners in the race, cheering them on, letting them know they can make it to the finish—and, of course, handing them that bottle of Living Water. Take it!

--Susan Parsons Sumner

ACKNOWLEDGMENTS

Acknowledgements are one of the easiest things to write in this book. Giving thanks out of a grateful heart to those who have helped you along the way is a blessing in itself.

First of all, of course, I must thank my Heavenly Father for his forgiveness, mercy, grace, faithfulness, patience, longsuffering with me. The path He has led me on has been an adventure I wouldn't trade with anyone. I am blessed and have seen His Hand continuously. There are not enough words of gratitude to express myself to Him and about Him.

Next, I must acknowledge my parents. My four siblings and I were brought up in church and taught about Jesus our whole lives. Where would I be without that heritage? I hate to even think about what the enemy would have done with me. Thank you, Mom and Dad, for making sure we were in church to hear about Jesus.

The friends and family that God sent to walk along side me in this life to encourage me are countless. I have been so blessed. But there are a few that have been a great example to me, a great encouragement to me--and kept me from falling many times.

My brother, Bruce. Always there for me, to hear me, to talk to me, to love me, to encourage me. My sister, Melanie. Always giving of herself even when she didn't even have one ounce of energy to give. My brother-in-law, Rick. For encouragement to buckle down and do it…just plain buggin' me. My best friend, Deb. Loving me unconditionally, no matter what. My cousins, Laura and Tim. Always including me in their family, listening to me and blessing me in ways they don't even know. My cousins, Jen and Jared. There to do warfare for me. In the trenches with me. My great college buddies, Debbie and Sondra. You have loved me and shared your lives with me. My precious friend and mentor, Sherry. You taught me about healing and deliverance and brought me through so much. I am forever grateful. Sister in the faith, Jackie. Someone to run things by on a regular basis. Someone who hears God clearly and shares His Word. And, Karen. A special friend through the years who has been my prayer warrior. Thank you is just not enough to say. To all these special people, I give God thanks and pray multiplied blessings for you in this earthly realm and in the Kingdom of God.

The last person I want to thank is Susan Parsons Sumner. She has always been a great influence in my life, whether she knew it or not. I dared to try things because she encouraged me. Two things that she greatly influenced: music and writing. Those two things have brought me to many places in this life I would have never gone. Thank you, Susan.

PREFACE

I was encouraged by a good friend to "write a book." Those were her exact words. She gave no commentary on what I had written, but had read a few of my blogs and decided I had something to say to the world out there. That single comment was the nudge I needed to believe it could happen. I highly regarded her opinion because of her own wealth of knowledge, wisdom, and writing expertise. God had placed it in my heart years ago, and she helped confirm it for me. Since then, God has encouraged me and confirmed this direction through a few others who have great writing ability. So, "in the mouth of two or three witnesses, a thing is established" (2 Corinthians 13:1). I am proceeding with my first attempt at publishing some of my walk with God.

So, with prayer and guidance of the Holy Spirit, I am believing God will use these pages to minister to hearts and hopefully, not just "bless" someone, but "heal" them. Thank you for investing your time to read these pages of my personal insights and experiences walking this path of adventure with God.

INTRODUCTION
THE RACE

In *A Tale of Two Cities*, Charles Dickens has this to say:

"It was the best of times, it was the worst of times; it was the age of wisdom , it was the age of foolishness; it was the epoch of belief, it was the epoch of incredulity; it was the season of Light, it was the season of Darkness; it was the spring of hope, it was the winter of despair; we had everything before us, we had nothing before us; we were all going directly to Heaven, we were all going the other way."

That is how I could describe many years of my life. I know that most of you relate to that as well. Along with the bad comes the good. Along with the foolishness comes the wisdom. Along with the faithlessness comes the faith. Along with the darkness comes the Light. With the discouragement comes the hope.

Through it all, there comes a greater understanding of self, of others, of God and His love ... For that painful time, for that dark time, for that overwhelming time, I am grateful. Often when we are "in" the midst of it, we are not grateful. As we are going "through" it, we are not grateful. But God wants us to get to the place we can do just that--be grateful in whatever circumstance we are in, because we trust Him and know that He has allowed these things to build in us the character of Christ. Through all these disappointments, a new hope, and a new direction. As God's Word says, "And we know that all things work together for good to them that love God, to them who are the called according to His purpose" (Romans 8:28).

Every day is a new adventure and a new opportunity. Every time we go through and come out stronger, wiser, more faithful, more grateful, we have new and more potential to impact this world for the better. Each of us wants to be a good steward and a good servant to our God in Heaven with the time we have left on this earth.

> **Philippians 3:14**
> I **press toward** the mark for the **prize of the high calling of God** in Christ Jesus.
>
> **1 Corinthians 9:24**
> Know ye not that they which **run in a race** run all, but one receives **the prize?** So run, that ye may obtain.

Hebrews 12:1
Let us lay aside every weight, and the sin which doth so easily beset us, and let us **run with patience the race** that is set before us.

We have to focus on this endurance race. We have to press in and forward for that prize of the high calling of God. Many take that prize so lightly—but it is such an honor! After all, that's what this life is all about--pressing into relationship with God and on to the prize of honoring our God Who loves us beyond measure and desires for all His children to win this race. The prize offers unspeakable peace and satisfaction in this life, and hope for the life hereafter! To know God—really know Him—and to recognize His guidance, knowing that it always leads to good...there is no greater joy.

We have to keep blinders on to the carnivals and sideshows going on around us. We need to keep blinders on to the sparkle of the things of this world, the lust of the flesh, the lust of the eyes, the pride of life (1 John 2:16). We need to keep focused on our goal, our call to honor God with this life He has given us. We need to run the race. We need to get back up if we fall and keep going after we stumble.

We cannot pay attention to what others are saying about the falls or the stumbles. We need to press on toward the mark. We cannot be deterred from the Prize. No one said it would be easy. It is an uphill climb much of the way, but we go in His strength. We make it on His strength and our surrender.

In the pages of this book, may you find encouragement that you need to keep going strong. May you be encouraged to make changes and dig deeper and fly higher with Him.

1 Corinthians 9:24-25
Know ye not that they which run in a race run all, but one receiveth the prize? So run, that ye may obtain. And every man that striveth for the mastery is temperate in all things. Now **they *do it* to obtain a corruptible crown; but we an incorruptible.**

2 Timothy 4:8
Henceforth there is laid up for me **a crown of righteousness**, which the Lord, the righteous judge, shall give me at that day: and not to me only, but unto all them also that love his appearing.

THE POTTERY

One day as I was sitting in my house, minding my own business, I heard this horrible smash with multiple clanging sounds. My washer had been overloaded and unbalanced, therefore, causing the spin cycle to vibrate excessively and shake things up more than usual. Apparently, the vibration from the washer vibrated the refrigerator enough to cause a large piece of glazed pottery to walk right off the top. That was only possible because the refrigerator wasn't level.

While I was cleaning it up, I couldn't believe how far pieces scattered and how much of it there was! In my mind, there was no way that one piece of pottery could have taken that much clay and glaze material to make it! But, my mind knows that all the sum of the parts equal the whole. So, it all had to be from the same piece of pottery.

I was able to clean it up without help, but it took some time to find those small splintered shards. Clean-up didn't happen all in one day either. I kept finding little shards throughout the next few weeks. I was aware they were probably there, and then, sure enough, I would see something glistening in the light. It was easy to spot them when the light reflected off them.

It was very important to cover a large area to pick up even the tiniest of shards, because those are the ones that can hurt and go in so deeply to the bottom of your feet. Even worse, your shards may get into the feet of your friends.

When your feet are in pain, you can't walk very well. You can't accomplish what you had intended to accomplish or finish the work you were supposed to do if your feet are in pain and you can't walk properly. That's a good reason to have someone help us clean up the mess. Another pair of eyes is always better, because they can see things that we sometimes can't see. They are standing in a different position. The light is reflecting from a different angle. They can pick it up, because they are positioned differently. They may be taller or shorter or standing just right in the reflective light. You really want to prevent those shards from imbedding in your feet or the feet of your friends.

This all brought to mind how we sometimes look at things in our lives. Many times things fall apart in our lives and look so big and seem to spread so far into other areas or our lives and the lives of others. We can't even see the far reaching effects because we haven't been in the right position with the "reflective Light" to see properly.

Even small splinters can be very painful if we don't clean it up properly. We can easily see the big pieces and take care of them, but it's the tiny shards, those small "foxes that spoil the vine" (**Song of Solomon 2:15**) that are sometimes hard to see without another pair of eyes. Because we weren't able to get all the shards, we step on a few here and there and cause ourselves or our friends some hurt. Then, we definitely need another pair of eyes to find the shard that is causing so much pain. When things are exposed to the LIGHT, they are easier to spot.

Things often shatter when they are not level or balanced. This can happen to us spiritually as well. First of all, we need to try to stay balanced in our walk with the Lord, but sometimes things just don't go as we think they should or the way we had planned. The vibrations of life, the trials and adversities, can shake some things up in our lives to the point of causing us to crash. When we "crash", it seems overwhelming. We have to reach out for help when we're hurting.

Galatians 6:2 speaks to this:

> Bear one another's burdens and so fulfill the law of Christ.

When we can't seem to accomplish what we intended to accomplish, or be what we thought we should be, it's really our pain that keeps us from walking where we should walk. We need to look deeper inside and let the Lord search our hearts. We are more focused on the "why" we can't get where we're going than on the "how" can we get where we're going. The "why" is because we're wounded and need healing to walk properly before God and man. The "how" is to reach out to our brothers and sisters for prayer, admonishing, and encouragement to be healed so we can walk the narrow path as God has intended.

> **James 5:16**
> Confess your faults one to another, and pray one for another, that ye may be healed. The effectual fervent prayer of a righteous man availeth much.

The healing comes with facing the situation, confessing, and prayer of our brothers and sisters in the Body of Christ. As long as the shards stay buried and you don't tell anyone they are there, they will remain buried and start to fester. This will only cause more pain and infection, spreading to other areas of your life and those around you. Sometimes it will work its way out with the festering. Sometimes God will allow "private" healing, but many times He uses us to help each other.

There are others in the Body of Christ that can see things from a different perspective for us. They have walked a different path, but serve the same Lord. Others hear the Holy Spirit more clearly than we do at times, and it's that discernment that can help set us free. Let someone help.

Do you want to have everyone see it and smell the festering? It's not a pretty sight and it's not a pretty situation. Do you want others to see that nasty side of things? It's at that point you will have to take antibiotics, some kind of care from someone else other than yourself. Why let it go that far? Deal with the pain before it festers. If you never get the help you need, and let it work itself to the point of exhaustion and discouragement, it can cause you to be crippled and scarred. You never had to let it get that far. Reach out for help from the Body of Christ. Let there be confession, repentance, submission and prayer for healing from your brothers and sisters in the Lord. Obey the Word and see its power in action.

You think you can walk this life alone? Not a chance.

We desperately need each other.

FLIGHT FEATHERS

In Psalm 91:4, we are told that God will cover us with His feathers and under His wings we may feel safe, trust and find refuge. Every time I would read that Scripture, another Scripture from Matthew 23:37 came to mind. It's when Jesus prayed over Israel saying how often He longed to "gather them under His wings like a mother hen would gather her chicks." I would picture this hen covering her chicks during the storms or in other times of danger. They are all cozy and protected, unaware of all that is really going on around them. They just knew they were safe and secure. This mind picture would give me a feeling of security and an assurance of the depth of His love I didn't feel at other times.

As I read that same Scripture again and again throughout my life, one day a completely different scenario flashed into my mind that made even more sense to me as a Christian trying to walk out this "salvation with fear and trembling" (Philippians 2:12). It was so encouraging and uplifting to my soul that I wanted to share it with others. We all need encouragement and any little bit helps. Other verses in that same Psalm connected the whole scene together for me as I had never seen before. It was like watching an enjoyable movie play out before my eyes.

For the purpose of my personal description of Psalm 91, let's focus on some of the highlighted phrases. Read the Psalm out loud so you hear it and build more faith.

> **Psalm 91**
> <u>1</u> He that dwelleth in the secret place of the most High **shall abide under the** shadow of the Almighty.
> <u>2</u> I will say of the LORD, **He is my refuge** and my fortress: my God; in him will I trust.
> <u>3</u> Surely **he shall deliver thee** from the snare of the fowler, *and* from the noisome pestilence.
> <u>4</u> He shall **cover thee with his feathers, and under his wings shalt thou trust:** his truth *shall be thy* shield and buckler.
> <u>5</u> Thou shalt not be afraid for the terror by night; *nor* for the arrow *that* flieth by day;
> <u>6</u> *Nor* for the pestilence *that* walketh in darkness; *nor* for the destruction *that* wasteth at noonday.
> <u>7</u> A thousand shall fall at thy side, and ten thousand at thy right hand; *but* it shall not come nigh thee.'
> <u>8</u> Only with thine eyes shalt thou behold and see the reward of the wicked.
> <u>9</u> Because thou hast made the LORD, *which is* my refuge, **even the most High, thy habitation;**
> <u>10</u> There shall no evil befall thee, neither shall any plague come nigh thy dwelling.
> <u>11</u> For he shall give his angels charge over thee, to keep thee in all thy ways.
> <u>12</u> They shall bear thee up in *their* hands, lest thou dash thy foot against a stone.
> <u>13</u> Thou shalt tread upon the lion and adder: the young lion and the dragon shalt thou trample under feet.

<u>14</u> Because he hath set his love upon me, therefore will I deliver him: **I will set him on high**, because he hath known my name.
<u>15</u> He shall call upon me, and I will answer him: I *will be* with him in trouble; I will deliver him, and honour him.
<u>16</u> With long life will I satisfy him, and shew him my salvation.

As I read other translations of the Bible, they included the words "feathers" and "pinions". So, the first thing I decided I needed to do was check out the function of "feathers" and "pinions". There was a difference in how "feathers" function and how "pinions" function.

The different sources were in agreement with the Wikipedia definition. So, we will appropriate their information here.

"Flight feathers" or "wings" are symmetrically paired and their **primary function is to aid in the generation of thrust and lift, thereby enabling flight**. Flight feathers can perform other functions: **territorial displays, courtship rituals, feeding methods**. The primaries are connected to the bird's manus or "hand". They can be rotated individually. These feathers are especially important for flapping flight, as they are the principal source of thrust. On the upstroke, when the bird often draws its wing in close to the body, the primaries are separated and rotated, reducing air resistance while still providing some thrust. The flexibility on the wingtips of large soaring birds allows for the spreading of the feathers which helps to reduce the creation of wingtip vortices, thereby reducing drag. The **pinion is the outermost part of the primary wing. The pinion is connected to the phalanges.**

For those who don't know, phalanges are like our fingers. The birds are able to move them individually or in unison to accomplish what they need to accomplish, just as we humans.

As the Scripture says, He is not only covering us with His feathers, but He is covering us with His "pinions". With the definition in mind and the information provided about being in flight, we can look at this in quite a different way. Pinions are the most flexible parts of the wings. They help maneuver the bird wherever he wants to go. They were meant to keep the bird maneuvering and moving, which also "protects" the bird by getting him out of harm's way.

So, here's where the new revelation came into focus for me. This visual helped encourage my heart and hopefully will encourage you as well. In my mind's eye, I see Jesus as a hang-glider with me riding tandem with Him. I'm strapped securely to Him. He is soaring up and down the currents of the air over His creation. I am "fixed and stable" with Him as He is controlling the wings and the flight. I am depending on Him to steer and trusting that He knows what He is doing and where He is taking me. I am under His wings, under His shadow, under His direction, under His protection. He is moving the apparatus to maneuver where He wants to go, where He wants to take me, where I can see much more of what is going on than if I was on earth. I am "on high" with Him. I am under His wings and have refuge from all the earthly things going on below me. I am separated from it all, but still a part of it all. I am seeing things from a complete different perspective. Everything looks smaller from that vantage point. You can see much more of the picture from that position. So it seems that the closer we are to Him, the smaller the things of this world, the cares of our personal world, will seem.

Not only am I "seeing" things from a different perspective, I am "feeling" things differently as well. The adventure of catching the different winds, changing directions, gliding from one scenario to the next without rapid, uncontrolled descent…the freedom and exhilaration of such a ride I can't imagine. Is that what this Christian walk is really supposed to be? A walk of freedom and exhilaration like no other? A walk that really is a ride? A ride where we are strapped in safe, secure, protected, loved, directed by the wind of the Holy Spirit? I do believe so.

Could it be that as we are "under His Wings" we are soaring in the secret place of the Most High? We are soaring above all those things: the terror of night, the arrow, the pestilence, the destruction. When we lean on Him and rely on Him, we are protected from the negative effects of the things that happen. Protected in the sense expressed by the Apostle Paul; "…and none of these things move me" (Acts 20:24). Not the terror of night, the arrow, the pestilence, the destruction. The only thing that "moves me" is the wind of the Spirit as I'm strapped on, fixed and stable, to my Savior.

As I stay in His secret place, remain covered with His feathers, remain under His shadow, no matter what the circumstances are, I will keep soaring. I will keep moving where He moves, and glide where He glides. I will let nothing distract me from what I am to do and where I am to go, because I am fixed and stable in Him. I am a spectator to so much that is going on in this world now, where I had been participating way too much before. I am not as accessible to the enemy anymore. I see things from a different perspective now. Those things no longer affect me.

Don't we all need refuge under His Wings? Don't we all need to soar above it all? Don't we need to see things from a different perspective?

There was another part of the definition for flight feathers from Wikipedia that also piqued my interest. It says that the flight feathers perform for other reasons as well: **territorial displays, courtship rituals, feeding methods**.

The various definitions made me think of many other things that our God is to us. It tells us how God is showing us His territory when we are under His Wings. He tells us in Psalm 24:1 that the earth is His and everything that dwells there. He is showing us His territory as He maneuvers His wings around His creation. He is showing us that there is nothing that we can't rise above. He is showing us that as long as we stay strapped in with Him, He will show us things that we can't even imagine. He will take us places that no mind could conceive. Adventure. That's what He will give us.

He is showing us that we are protected by Him and following His every move. Nowhere else can we be so in line with Him as when we are under His Wings. He is there, fixed and stable. He is protecting and leading us in the right direction, maneuvering through the territory of our lives so we get the best perspective on things. We, in turn, are leaning on and trusting Him to take us to and through the right areas in the right way in the right time. We are safe and He is providing His strength, His protection, His love, His direction for us all along the way.

His "feeding methods". He is providing our sustenance the whole time. He is keeping us strong in our spirit as we stay strapped in with His Spirit. He is maneuvering our life His way, so we get the right spiritual nutrition to grow properly. He makes sure we go to the proper feeding grounds for the right spiritual food…if we stay strapped in with Him. Keep strapped in so you don't wander to the wrong feeding grounds.

When the definition also talks about "courtship rituals", we have to keep in mind that we are His Bride. In this scenario, He is being our perfect Husband and lover of our soul: protecting, providing, giving direction, giving us everything we need to be close to Him and be in the same rhythm of life.

So, the next time you are overwhelmed…strap yourself in "the secret place of the Most High"--"in the shadow of the Almighty" and glide above it all in His presence with His flight feathers in control.

Walk in the Spirit.

ARE WE SKATING BY?

As I watched the ice skaters in the Winter Olympics, I was amazed at their strength and stamina. What amazed me even more is how they get back up when they fall, and they just keep going to finish their program or course. There doesn't even appear to be a hiccough in their program. They don't let it deter them from finishing their course.

> **Proverbs 24:16**
> For a just man falls seven times, and rises up again.
>
> **Psalm 37:24**
> Though he fall, he shall not be utterly cast down: for the Lord upholds him with his hand.
>
> **1 Corinthians 9:24**
> Know ye not that they which run in a race run all, but one receives the prize? So run, that ye may obtain.

The skaters know that even though they've made mistakes, they get credit if they keep going. The score isn't all based on the mistakes. Someone is keeping score of each individual performance. They aren't getting compared to another skater. They are being compared to the qualifications and standards of the sport.

> **2 Timothy 2:5**
> Also, if anyone competes as an athlete, he does not win the prize unless he competes according to the rules.

How many times have we compared ourselves to others or to our own performance, when it's not about that at all. It's about God's standards. It's about God's definitions of life in His Word. He doesn't "keep score" like we do. His perspective of our performance is love-based.

The skaters don't get high scores for just skating around and not doing anything that is seen of value to the judges. They can't expect to win a prize if they just skate around with no real skill and accomplishing nothing. They have to do things that took a great deal of practice and more practice.

They have to do things their coaches ask them to do, even when they think it's impossible. They have to try over and over and over again to accomplish the greater feats. They have to build their strength consistently and continually and with much practice. To get the high scores and the great reward, they have to "do" feats that seem impossible to many of us. They train and train and try and try again and again to accomplish those great leaps and spins and stretches. They don't give up. They have faith that their consistent strengthening and practice will pay off in the end.

> **James 2:26**
> For as the body apart from the spirit is dead, even so faith apart from works is dead.
>
> **Hebrews 11:6**
> But without faith it is impossible to please him: for he that cometh to God must believe that he is, and that he is a rewarder of them that diligently seek him.

The skaters push themselves beyond their limits, it seems. They don't let a stumble or fall distract them. By faith, they keep doing the feats that they practiced over and over again. They know they have built their strength. They leap by faith that their strength and practice will pay off. They have to keep going. They are headed for the GOLD!

> **Philippians 3:14**
> I press toward the mark for the prize of the high calling of God in Christ Jesus.

They are focused on one thing: finishing the course to obtain the award.

> **2 Timothy 4:7**
> I have fought a good fight, I have finished my course, I have kept the faith.

It's not enough to be on the skates. It's not enough just to say you have Jesus as your Savior. You have to build up strength and stamina to qualify to be a contender in the sport and skate according to the rules. You have to hunger and thirst after righteousness (Matthew 5:6) to be filled and run this race for the prize.

It's not all about "winning" and "being the best", it's about giving, working, trying, believing. It's about fulfilling your course. It's about consistently pressing in to Him, hungering, thirsting for Him, focusing on Him as our everything so that our soul and spirit will soar beyond limits we imagined.

Don't just "skate by" in this life. Be the champion skater. Get up time after time and finish the course. Give it all you have. Do it all for the Prize. Surrender it all to Jesus. Keep pushing. Keep crucifying that flesh daily, moment by moment.

> **Galatians 5:24**
> And they that are Christ's have crucified the flesh with the affections and lusts.

And keep your armor on to do warfare with any obstacles that are in the way to bring glory to God and honor to His Name. Keep on the right equipment to fulfill the course. Skaters need skates, but we need so much more equipment than that in this race for the Prize.

In **Ephesians 6:11-18** we are told how to live and work within our temporary abiding places: the flesh and this world.

> Put on the whole armor of God, that ye may be able to stand against the wiles of the devil. For we wrestle not against flesh and blood, but against principalities, against powers, against the rules of the darkness of this world, against spiritual wickedness in high places. Wherefore take unto you the whole armor of God, that ye may be able to withstand in the evil day, and having done all, to stand. Stand therefore, having your loins girt about with truth, and having on the breastplate of righteousness; And your feet shod with the preparation of the gospel of peace; Above all, taking the shield of faith, wherewith ye shall be able to quench all the fiery darts of the wicked. And take the helmet of salvation, and the Sword of the Spirit, which is the Word of God: Praying always with all prayer and supplication in the Spirit, and watching thereunto with all perseverance and supplication for all saints.

This whole race comes down to this…It's not just about us. It's doing it for our brothers and sisters, for the Kingdom of God. Just like the athletes represent their country, we are a part of each other. What we do affects the honor of the whole. We are to reflect the image of His Son to the world and each other to bring glory and honor to Him that we may win some.

You are still a skater, still in this Olympics, still in the family of God, but will not receive the greatest reward and will not please the Father if you don't follow the regulations and rules…being obedient to His Word. You say, "why do I need a reward or win the prize?" Again, it's not about you! It's for the Glory of God. Not for your glory. It's all about bringing honor to His Name, not to yourself. It's about building His Kingdom. It's about expressing your love for the One Who loved you above measure and gave everything for you.

2 Timothy 4:8
Henceforth there is laid up for me a crown of righteousness, which the Lord, the righteous judge, shall give me at that day: and not to me only, but unto all them also that love his appearing.

Revelation 4:10-11
The four and twenty elders fall down before Him that sat on The Throne, and worship Him that lives for ever and ever, and cast their crowns before The Throne, saying, Thou art worthy, O Lord, to receive glory and honor and power: for Thou hast created all things, and for Thy pleasure they are and were created.

Don't just skate by. Be an Olympian!

COMMUNICATING IS SUCH A SACRIFICE!

There is a particular Scripture that hit me with new revelation that I'd like to share with you. It was one of those "aha!" moments. It really started turning the wheels in my head. I began relating it to my real life experiences, giving me a whole new understanding, showing me an area in my life that needed some repair. What I dug out of the Scriptures regarding these two verses is a little correction, instruction and reproof for righteousness sake (2 Timothy 3:16).

> **Hebrews 13:15-16**
> 15 By Him therefore let us offer the sacrifice of praise to God continually, that is, the fruit of our lips giving thanks to His Name.
> 16 But to do good and to communicate forget not: for with such sacrifices God is well pleased.

So, what are the sacrifices here? Praising, doing good, and communicating. Let's focus on "communicating" as a sacrifice to God.

I think of communicating as an investment of time and energy, and sometimes, let's face it, a real hassle. Sometimes it's easier to do it yourself than to communicate what needs to be done or said. We don't want to bother with it or expend the energy to communicate to the depth or extent we may need to do. God's Word tells us we need to do this to please Him. Yet, we are reluctant to take time and energy many times to do just that…communicate.

Communicate in the Greek for this particular verse is "koinonia", which means to communicate, fellowship, communion, partnership, participation, distribution (*Strong's Exhaustive Concordance of the Bible*).

The internet is very helpful with definitions as well. I will use www.thefreedictionary.com to uncover some great meanings to the words we use.

1 - to convey information about: make known; impart knowledge or exchange thoughts, feelings, or ideas
2 - to spread to others; transmit as in an infectious disease/virus; to transfer
3 - to have an interchange, as of ideas
4 - to express oneself in such a way that one is readily and clearly understood
5 - to be connected with one another; to make or have a connecting passage or route; to connect or join

Aren't there people that you have cut off communication with because it's way too much work?...way too much hassle?...way too much energy?...you are too tired to take time for someone?...too busy to keep up relationships?...too tired or busy to attend or plan times of fellowship?

Maybe we've been hurt, so we avoid communication. We think it saves us from more hurt, yet, because we are God's creations, created for relationship, we're shooting ourselves in the foot on this one. We are His family. We cannot live without communion, fellowship, communication, and relationship with one another and Him and expect to be healthy in body, soul, and spirit. There are so many unhealthy believers for just this reason.

God brings people across our paths on purpose that He wants us to "communicate" with for some reason. We need to embrace the opportunities to "please" God. And, "communicating" pleases Him well. We are "to be connected" and convey information, impart knowledge and be infectious, transferring our infection of God's love, grace and mercy to each other.

The second most important word we need to look at from these verses is **sacrifice**.

Sacrifice
Noun:
1 - the act of offering, losing, surrendering something to a deity in propitiation or homage
2 - forfeiture of something highly valued for the sake of one considered to have a great value or claim
3 - relinquishment of something at less than its presumed value
4 - a loss entailed by giving up
5 - the act of killing
6 - in baseball, an "out" that advances the base runners

Verb:
1 - to forfeit one thing for another thing considered to be of great value
2 - to endure the loss of
3 - to give away for the sake of something or someone else
4 - to dedicate, to give thought to, to give priority to, to pay attention, to kill or destroy
5 - sell at a loss
6 - in baseball, make a sacrifice bunt or sacrifice fly
7 - in chess, to permit or force one's opponent to capture a piece freely

Sacrifice as a noun and a verb: surrendering, relinquishing, forfeiting, offering, the act of killing, all speak to our walk with God. Surrendering our hearts and lives to Him. Relinquishing our claim on anything. Forfeiting our dreams and desires for His dreams and desires for us. Offering ourselves daily by crucifying our flesh. Killing or quenching the fleshly desires and magnetic pull on our lives

As I pondered this Scripture and each definition of the key words, sacrifice and communication, it opened my mind and heart to a new and, hopefully, deeper understanding.

The definition of sacrifice that stood out like a bolt to me was: in baseball, an "out" that advances the base runners. If we put ourselves "out" or "sacrifice", it would advance the runners! Aren't we all runners in this race? The sacrifice to honor God by obeying His Word advances the runners. Wow!

Let's see what the Word of God says about the runners on base in the game of life.

> **1 Corinthians 9:24**
> Know ye not that they which run in a race run all, but one receives the prize? So run, that ye may obtain.
>
> **Philippians 2:16**
> Holding forth the Word of Life; that I may rejoice in the Day of Christ, that I have not run in vain, neither labored in vain.
>
> **Hebrews 12:1**
> Wherefore seeing we also are compassed about with so great a cloud of witnesses, let us lay aside every weight, and the sin which doth so easily beset us, and let us run with patience the race that is set before us.

Does the schedule you keep please God? If you aren't fitting in the communication, fellowship, participation, relationships, etc., how can you be pleasing God? He asks us to praise Him, do good, and communicate. That's what pleases Him.

Pleasing God should be always foremost in our minds and hearts. Let's read a few more Scriptures about pleasing Him. Let them sink into your soul and spirit. Memorize them. Meditate on them. You will then know how to please the Father.

> **Hebrews 11:6**
> But without faith it is impossible to please Him: for He that cometh to God must believe that He is, and that He is a rewarder of them that diligently seek Him.

Pleasing Him is having faith in Him. Pleasing Him is believing His Word and His Voice. Pleasing Him is trusting that He will fulfill all that He said He would. Pleasing Him is not getting weary in well-doing. We also know that faith without works is dead. So pleasing Him is "doing by faith".

> **Hebrews 13:16**
> But to do good and to communicate forget not: for with such sacrifices God is well pleased.

The sacrifice of "doing" good and "communicating" please the Father.

> **Proverbs 16:7**
> When a man's ways please the Lord, He makes even his enemies to be at peace with him.

Pleasing the Father will cause your enemies to be at peace with you! AND, pleasing Him will make it easier for you to deal with things that come your way, because you will be relying on Him and trusting Him.

> **Romans 8:8**
> So then they that are in the flesh cannot please God.

Walking in the Spirit is what pleases God, not walking in the flesh. When you walk in the Spirit, you are in step with Him, walking where He walks, going where He goes, seeing what He sees. You have wisdom and discernment to function the way you were meant to function.

> **2 Timothy 2:4**
> No man that wars entangles himself with the affairs of this life; that he may please Him Who has chosen him to be a soldier.

Keeping our eyes on prize for the high calling of Jesus Christ. Keeping our treasures in heavenly things and not earthly things. Not entangling ourselves with the pride of life, lust of the eye, lust of the flesh. Being free to do His bidding. Being free to go and not be tied to any earthly thing. The affairs of this life keep us too sidetracked, too entangled to be "on the ready" for God's bidding.

Communicate. Make the effort. Put yourself "out". Sacrifice. Be ready to give an answer to any man that asks. Listen for the bidding of the Holy Spirit.

> **1 Peter 3:15**
> But sanctify the Lord God in your hearts: and *be* ready always to *give* an answer to every man that asketh you a reason of the hope that is in you with meekness and fear:

Advance the runners!

DEN OF THIEVES

As I was reading in the book of Matthew, I came across part of two verses that I'd never heard anyone preach on before in the way I perceived them. That doesn't mean someone hasn't tackled it, but I'd never heard it. It stuck in my head and my heart. I had to go back to it and dig into it a little deeper.

> **Matthew 21:12-13**
> **12** And Jesus went into the temple of God, and cast out all them that sold and bought in the temple, and overthrew the tables of the moneychangers, and the seats of them that sold doves, **13** And said unto them, it is written, My house shall be called the house of prayer; but ye have made it a den of thieves.

There are two phrases in this Scripture passage that I've never heard anyone address:

1 - "…and cast out **ALL** them that **SOLD and BOUGHT** in the temple."

2 - "…**YE** have made it a **DEN OF THIEVES**."

Why those who **BOUGHT** in the temple? The Scripture says He cast them **ALL** out… ALL that **sold and bought**. By the Law of Moses, given by God, and by Jewish tradition, they were expected to **BRING a sacrifice TO** the temple to have the priest make a sacrifice for their sins. Instead of making preparation and bringing God their best, many were settling for whatever was available at the last minute. They weren't taking this seriously. It had become very "routine" for them. They weren't prepared in their hearts for true repentance or worship. They weren't prepared to worship Him as a Holy God deserved.

I'm thinking Christ was disgusted with those who were lazy worshipers. That's why he cast out ALL who sold and bought. They were **ROBBING** God of His deserved honor and worship there in the **"den of thieves"**. They were disrespecting His provision for them... forgiveness of sin... and so much more.

When you want to honor someone, don't you shop for just the right card? Don't you shop for just the right gift? Don't you make effort to think and prepare to do something to honor them, to bless them? Isn't your mind focused on who they have been to you, what they are going through, or what a blessing they have been to others? Are you not thinking about them and all their attributes? As you focus on them, this endears them even more to your heart and makes you endeavor to get just the right thing or do that special thing to bring them joy and pleasure. God deserves such attention. He deserves our time and effort. He deserves our preparation. He deserves our meditation.

The Bible tells us "to give honor to whom honor" is due (Romans 13:7). When someone has been a great blessing in many lives, don't they hold big celebrations of honor? Doesn't God deserve our honor more than any man? When we gather together, isn't that what we're supposed to do? Isn't that what "church" is about? To bring God honor as His Body, to celebrate Him, to offer Him our sacrifice of praise (Hebrews 13:15) and worship?

Everything in the Old Testament was a shadow of things to come. Didn't the priests of old have a high price to pay for not preparing as instructed? They had to be clean and wash a certain way and dress a certain way, all representing Jesus' sacrifice, His holiness and the cleansing of His Blood. The priests' lives were required of them when they did not prepare and honor God as instructed. We are priest and kings in His Kingdom here on earth. Much is required of us as well. This is a very sobering Scripture truth.

> **Romans 12:1**
> I beseech you therefore brethren by the mercies of God that you present your bodies a living sacrifice, holy, acceptable unto God, which is your reasonable service.

Since we no longer bring animals for sacrifice, because Jesus was the Ultimate Sacrifice, we are instructed to be LIVING SACRIFICES. Since we no longer need an earthly priest to stand between us and God, because Jesus is our High Priest (Hebrews 3-7) and Mediator between God and man (1 Timothy 2:5), don't we need to prepare our hearts?

I'm thinking He's not very happy with lazy worshipers. And I'm thinking there is a price to pay for not preparing our hearts and worshiping Him "in spirit and in truth" (John 4:24).

Be ready to worship!

HOW VITAL ARE YOU IN THE KINGDOM OF GOD?

In 2 Kings we read about a great commander of the armies named Naaman. He was a high ranking official, a captain in the army, and in today's army, may have even been ranked a general. And then, there was his wife's little maid. You'll need to read the rest of the chapter to get the whole story, but these three verses will get the point across.

> **2 Kings 5:1-3**
> Now Naaman, captain of the host of the king of Syria, was a great man with his master, and honourable, because by him the Lord had given deliverance unto Syria: he was also a mighty man in valour, but he was a leper.
> And the Syrians had gone out by companies, and had brought away captive out of the land of Israel a little maid; and she waited on Naaman's wife.
> And she said unto her mistress, Would God my lord were with the prophet that is in Samaria! For he would recover him of his leprosy.

His wife's maid was a "servant". What even seems worse, she was brought captive out of her homeland and sent to be a servant in unfamiliar territory and a different culture. She was removed from all her family, friends and comforts of home. And, in the midst of her circumstances appearing to be horrible, this was actually a promotion in God's Kingdom, because God had an assignment for her. She didn't get into this "position" by chance. She was good at her job, no matter how menial it may have seemed to those on the outside looking in. If she hadn't been there and been obedient to do her "assignment" by using her gifts and abilities, things may have turned out quite differently. God knew she was the one who would be obedient and fulfill this task for Him. Her steps were ordered of the Lord. She had an assignment.

> **Psalm 37:23**
> The steps of a good man are ordered by the Lord: and He delighteth in his way.

Sometimes we are in "positions" that we resist. You tell yourself it's too menial. I have more to offer… blah, blah, blah. It could actually be a promotion in the Kingdom of God. Does God have an assignment for you? Yes. Has He given you this position to accomplish a mission for the Kingdom? Yes. There are no mistakes when He has ordered your steps.

> **Acts 17:26-27**
> And He made from one common origin, one source, one blood, all nations of men to settle on the face of the earth, having definitely determined their allotted periods of time and the fixed boundaries of their habitation, their settlements, lands, and abodes, so that they should seek God, in the hope that they might feel after Him and find Him, although He is not far from each one of us.

This is my favorite Scripture of all time. When I felt lost and out of place, I read those verses. When things didn't fit in my life, I read those verses. When nothing fell in line as expected, I read those verses. He was placing me in position to seek after Him. The circumstances of my life caused me to seek after Him.

We are in the "place" and "time" where He has placed us. God assigns you your residence. You don't choose where to live. He knows where you will seek Him the most. One translation says that we would "grope" after Him as in desperately groping for something in the dark. He places us in time, place, and circumstances so that we will "grope" after Him, to seek after Him.

He wants us dependent on Him. He wants to give us direction and assignments where we are, in the midst of sometimes overwhelming circumstances.

This little handmaiden didn't have a personal agenda here. She really didn't seek for personal significance. She spoke from her heart and shared it with even those to whom she was subservient. His "position" didn't hinder her from helping. His "predicament" spurred her on to help. She had a servant's heart.

If we ever think that our personal agenda will accomplish things for God - *Not*. If we ever think we need to have personal significance in our work for the Lord - *Not*. We are to be His vessel to use wherever He places us for His agenda and significance.

No matter where you are and what you are doing, God has an assignment for you. It may seem small, but may accomplish much. Naaman was used by God to win battles. He was a mighty warrior and was gifted of God as a leader. Had he not been healed, what good would he have been to God's purpose? Had the little maid not obeyed God, Naaman would have lost position and ultimately died. His country would have lost battles and suffered great loss. You tell me the little maid didn't have a big assignment? Her obedience saved the nation.

How important are you to God's Kingdom? You never know. Just be obedient where you are.

Leave a legacy for the Glory of God.

WHO GUARDS THE SHEPHERD?

In 1 Samuel, we see a principle that applies to our lives today, but many feel free to ignore or don't have spiritual understanding in the matter. It is very important to understand that honoring authority is high on God's priority list.

> **1 Samuel 26:1-16**
> 1 And the Ziphites came unto Saul to Gibeah, saying, Doth not David hide himself in the hill of Hachilah, which is before Jeshimon? ² Then Saul arose, and went down to the wilderness of Ziph, having three thousand chosen men of Israel with him, to seek David in the wilderness of Ziph. ³ And Saul pitched in the hill of Hachilah, which is before Jeshimon, by the way. But David abode in the wilderness, and he saw that Saul came after him into the wilderness. ⁴ David therefore sent out spies, and understood that Saul was come in very deed. ⁵ And David arose, and came to the place where Saul had pitched: and David beheld the place where Saul lay, and Abner the son of Ner, the captain of his host: and Saul lay in the trench, and the people pitched round about him. ⁶ Then answered David and said to Ahimelech the Hittite, and to Abishai the son of Zeruiah, brother to Joab, saying, Who will go down with me to Saul to the camp? And Abishai said, I will go down with thee. ⁷ So David and Abishai came to the people by night: and, behold, Saul lay sleeping within the trench, and his spear stuck in the ground at his bolster: but Abner and the people lay round about him. ⁸ Then said Abishai to David, God hath delivered thine enemy into thine hand this day: now therefore let me smite him,

I pray thee, with the spear even to the earth at once, and I will not smite him the second time. ⁹ And David said to Abishai, Destroy him not: **for who can stretch forth his hand against the LORD's anointed, and be guiltless?** ¹⁰ David said furthermore, As the LORD liveth, the LORD shall smite him; or his day shall come to die; or he shall descend into battle, and perish. ¹¹ **The LORD forbid that I should stretch forth mine hand against the LORD's anointed**: but, I pray thee, take thou now the spear that is at his bolster, and the cruse of water, and let us go. ¹² So David took the spear and the cruse of water from Saul's bolster; and they gat them away, and no man saw it, nor knew it, neither awaked: **for they were all asleep; because a deep sleep from the LORD was fallen upon them.** ¹³ Then David went over to the other side, and stood on the top of an hill afar off; a great space being between them: ¹⁴ And David cried to the people, and to Abner the son of Ner, saying, Answerest thou not, Abner? Then Abner answered and said, Who art thou that criest to the king? ¹⁵ **And David said to Abner, Art not thou a valiant man? and who is like to thee in Israel? wherefore then hast thou not kept thy lord the king? for there came one of the people in to destroy the king thy lord. ¹⁶ This thing is not good that thou hast done. As the LORD liveth, ye are worthy to die, because ye have not kept your master, the LORD's anointed. And now see where the king's spear is, and the cruse of water that was at his bolster.**

The statement that is the center of this whole passage is in verse 16: "What you have done is not good. As surely as the Lord lives, you and your men deserve to die, **because you did not guard your master, the Lord's anointed**". Wow! You deserve to die!!??!! Sounds like serious business to me. Sounds like serious business to God. We are held accountable to God to guard those in authority over us.

Romans 13:1-2 is clear on the matter of authority:

> 1 Let every person be subject to the governing authorities. For there is no authority except from God, and those that exist have been instituted by God.
> 2 Therefore whoever resists the authorities resists what God has appointed, and those who resist will incur judgment… give honor to whom honor is due.

Honor means high respect, as for worth, merit, or rank; to be held in honor (Webster's dictionary).

Resisting authority here in Romans 13 doesn't mean that you do everything no matter what. Our examples are Shadrach, Meshach, and Abednego. They wouldn't bow to the gods of the land even though the king commanded it. You have to honor God number one. All other authorities fall into place after honoring God and His Word.

You can "respectfully" honor them without agreeing with them. That is the same as with our parents. The Word tells us to "honor" our parents in Deuteronomy 5:16 and Ephesians 6:2. That's the only verse with such a great promise. The Word tells us that "our days will be long and things will go well with us". We don't have to agree with everything, but honor their position as God has chosen them to give you a place in this earth and His Kingdom.

Leadership and authority are flesh as we all are. We all "sin and come short of the glory of God" (**Romans 3:23**). The onslaught of the enemy is many times harder on those in leadership. They need us in their corner. They need us to pray for them and be on guard for the onslaught they have coming their way.

Have we dishonored God's appointed and anointed?

Have we disrespected those that God put in authority over us?

What have we done to protect them spiritually even when we haven't agreed with them?

Have we encouraged them in the Lord?

Have we prayed for them?

> **1 Timothy 2:1-3** even tells us why we need to pray for those in authority.
> 1 I exhort you therefore, that, first of all, supplications, prayers, intercessions, and giving of thanks, be made for all men.
> 2 For kings, and for all that are in authority: that we may lead a quiet and peaceable life in all godliness and honesty.
> 3 For this is good and acceptable in the sight of God our Savior;

Have we loved them and treated them also as a brother or sister in Christ?

Have we borne their burdens (**Galatians 6:2**)?

Have we been Aaron and Hur to them? Lifting up their arms in the heat of the battle?

Have we done warfare for them? (**Ephesians 6:10-18**)?

Have we stood in their corner through their failures (**James 5:16**)?

Or have we deserted them?

Have we helped to restore?

David is our example. He did his best to honor God's authority over him. He didn't cross that line of disrespect. He left it in God's hands. AND, in the natural or flesh, we would agree he deserved to take revenge. Saul was evil to him on so many levels for so many years. Yet, David fought battles for Saul. He killed Saul's enemies. He sang and played music for Saul to calm his spirit, to lift him up and encourage him. David used all his gifts and talents to honor the

King. He also knew when he had to leave. That is the reality in many of our lives. There is a time to leave… without dishonoring the other person's authority.

There have been untold millions of church splits and church relationship issues. If you've been in a church for any length of time, you have seen it and/or been a part of it at one time or another. So many times, things have not been handled according to God's Word to the detriment of the Church and the Body. God was never allowed to handle it His way. People got too antsy to get things done their way. God cannot honor that and many have seen the results of their decisions: *no good fruit*.

There were many times after "leaving" that David had to stay in a stronghold for protection. But there was a time that he left the stronghold to go into the land of Judah (**1 Samuel 22:5**). The Prophet Gad came to him to tell him to go, go into the land of PRAISE.

As we see in David's example, there was a time to leave the "stronghold" and go to the land of Judah or "praise". Resting and waiting until God's timing was fulfilled in both lives. Even doing it God's way, it still wasn't a pretty sight. What transpired in the following years, with the transition of the throne wasn't easy or fun for anyone. But God's timing was of utmost importance to accomplish what He wanted to accomplish. In the meantime, David still honored those in authority over him.

There will be those times in all our lives. We won't always be in agreement with authority. We won't want to move the way they may want us to move. Remember, God has assignments for us. God has places for us to be at different times in our lives. God wants us to hear Him clearly before we move. And, even David had to hear from God through a prophet. God will send others your way to help you hear more clearly. Many times when you are in the midst of it all, you can't hear as clearly as you should. God gave us each other to help us through.

God's timing is everything. He knows that sometimes we need protection. Sometimes we need to be out of the way for a while. But, He sends those along side of us to give direction, to give comfort, to give instruction. The best thing the Prophet Gad did was tell him to leave the bondage and go into PRAISE… from the stronghold to Judah! That's the place we need to be in the midst of it all as well.

God holds us accountable to "guard the shepherd". We may have to do it from a distance, but let us honor God by doing so.

> **1 Samuel 26:9**
> David said to Abishai, Do not destroy him; for who can raise his hand against the Lord's anointed and be guiltless?

Help guard those in authority. God will honor you.

PAIN

I've worked in hospitals and clinics for years as a nurse and nurse practitioner. I've heard many cries of pain. Each cry tugs at your heart strings. I've even caused some of those cries of pain by giving a shot or cleaning a wound, but it was all for the patient's good.

I heard somewhere, from someone much wiser than me, that there is a big difference between the cry coming from the cancer ward and the cry coming from the maternity ward. If I heard a gut-wrenching scream in the hospital, it made a difference where it came from… the cancer ward or the maternity ward: one is life and one is death. It gives us a little different perspective on things in life.

In our pain, many times we cannot tell the difference. The enemy of our souls wants us to think it's the cancer ward, but all the time the Holy Spirit wants us to know it's the maternity ward. God wants to birth something new in our spirit, in our lives, but the devil is trying to discourage us, trying to get us to hook into the belief we are in the cancer ward.

Many times God is trying to clean a wound and stitch us up. God wants to get us to understand that we will be much better after the wound is cleaned up and the healing process begins. Just as in the medical field, if we left the bacteria and dirt in the wound, it would never heal. If we never brought the edges of the wound back together to heal from the inside out, it would never be healed. It would get infection and begin to fester. Then this would call for big doses of strong antibiotics. Sometimes, the wound would even have to be reopened, scraping off the old, dying tissue so that it could be sewn back together again and begin proper healing yet again.

It's better to surrender to God's healing touch, even though painful at times, at the hands of those that love us, than to repeat the healing process over and over again. God sends others to help us through with their discernment, wisdom, love, compassion. We need to let the Body minister to us, and we need to be available to minister to the Body.

Romans 8 is such a great chapter about this entire scenario. It's hard to even pick out one verse to discuss. Please read the whole chapter, and read it out loud. Listen to it from your own lips. Let it encourage your heart, let the spoken Word build your faith. Let the Holy Spirit teach you and plant this seed of His Word deep. I have highlighted some parts to **focus on in this chapter with regards to death the enemy wants us to believe and the life that God wants us to receive.**

> **Romans 8**
> 1 There is therefore now no condemnation to them which are in Christ Jesus, who walk not after the flesh, but after the Spirit. ² For the law of the Spirit of life in Christ Jesus hath made me free from the law of sin and death.
> 6 For to be carnally minded is death; but to be spiritually minded is life and peace.
> ⁷ Because the carnal mind is enmity against God: for it is not subject to the law of God, neither indeed can be. ⁸ So then they that are in the flesh cannot please God.
> ⁹ But ye are not in the flesh, but in the Spirit, if so be that the Spirit of God dwell in you. Now if any man have not the Spirit of Christ, he is none of his.
> ¹⁰ And if Christ be in you, the body is dead because of sin; but the Spirit is life because of righteousness. ¹¹ But if the Spirit of him that raised up Jesus from the dead dwell in you, he that raised up Christ from the dead shall also quicken your mortal bodies by his Spirit that dwelleth in you.
> ¹² Therefore, brethren, we are debtors, not to the flesh, to

On To The Prize

live after the flesh. ¹³ For if ye live after the flesh, ye shall die: but if ye through the Spirit do mortify the deeds of the body, ye shall live.

¹⁸ For I reckon that the sufferings of this present time are not worthy to be compared with the glory which shall be revealed in us.

²⁸ And we know that all things work together for good to them that love God, to them who are the called according to his purpose.

³¹ What shall we then say to these things? If God be for us, who can be against us?

³⁴ Who is he that condemneth? It is Christ that died, yea rather, that is risen again, who is even at the right hand of God, who also maketh intercession for us.

³⁵ Who shall separate us from the love of Christ? shall tribulation, or distress, or persecution, or famine, or nakedness, or peril, or sword?

³⁶ As it is written, For thy sake we are killed all the day long; we are accounted as sheep for the slaughter.

³⁷ Nay, in all these things we are more than conquerors through him that loved us.

³⁸ For I am persuaded, that neither death, nor life, nor angels, nor principalities, nor powers, nor things present, nor things to come,

³⁹ Nor height, nor depth, nor any other creature, shall be able to separate us from the love of God, which is in Christ Jesus our Lord.

We need the Body of Christ to help us through it all. God made us relational beings, and we need each other to survive. We need to encourage each other in the battles of life. We need to be there for each other to help mend wounds and care for each other. I am my brother's keeper. We are to care for one another's souls. We are to do good, especially to those of "the household of faith".

Be a pain reliever.

REMEMBER NOAH

After many of the past events in my life, I would be discouraged about many things. I know you have been there, and you know what I'm talking about all too well. Discouraged because you have given and given and poured out and poured out for others without seeing any results of your labors. Makes one question many things within themselves. Am I really hearing God and obeying His Word?

We all want to be on track with God. But, there are always Job's comforters there to tell you what you did wrong and why this happened… blah, blah, blah. You've been on the receiving end of that, right? And, I'm sure we've all been a Job's comforter at one time or another in our spiritual immaturity. As I brought this before the Lord, as Psalm 142:2 says, "I poured my complaint out before the Lord." He just said to me, "Remember Noah".

So, I'm passing on to you what I heard. Noah just obeyed God. He was willing and obedient. He was going to do what God said and believed that God was going to take care of him and his family. He was trusting God with it all.

> **Isaiah 1:19**
> If ye be willing and obedient, ye shall eat the good of the land.

Noah didn't even have this Scripture to rely on. It was way after his time. He heard and obeyed.

No one "heard" what Noah had to say. No one was changed by what he preached or taught. No one encouraged him. No one was encouraged. No one helped him. He preached a tough message and preached it one hundred and twenty years! He continued on in his mission. He was obedient through it all. No matter what it looked like to other people. No matter who came against him. No matter who gossiped about him. No matter who slandered him. No matter who or what opposed him, Noah didn't let it deter him from what God had instructed. He kept plugging along day after day for one hundred and twenty years! But, the day came. The destiny of that mission came to fruition, suddenly.

Be encouraged. Remember Noah. It is our honor to be willing and obedient to God's Word and His bidding. The Almighty Creator communicates with us and wants to use us for His Kingdom purposes. We should be so grateful and honored. The outcome is in His hands. No matter who helps you or doesn't help you, no matter who doesn't encourage you, no matter who slanders you, no matter who gossips about you, no matter if you see fruit of your labors, no matter the opposition, keep being willing and obedient. Don't let circumstances deter you from being obedient to God's Word and the Holy Spirit's bidding. Continue to be willing and obedient.

This whole story and situation in my own life also reminded me of the Prophet Isaiah. God was looking for someone to give His Word to the nations. God said that whoever this person was would speak His Word, but no one would listen. God already warned him that no one would listen! Even knowing that information, Isaiah said, even so, send me.

Isaiah didn't worry about what people were going to say about him. Isaiah wasn't worried about what people would do to him. Isaiah didn't worry about the results or fruit of his labor. Isaiah was "willing and obedient". God promised him that he would eat the good of the land for his obedience. But God gave him that promise after he agreed to do God's bidding. God spoke promise and provision over Isaiah in the midst of it all.

Just like Isaiah, God had a promise and provision for Noah in his obedience. We are His children too. His promises are true for us as well. He is no respecter of persons (Acts 10:34). He promises to go with us and only asks for our obedience. Seems to me that we are the benefactor no matter what. The fruition we see for our labor may not be what fruition God intended for us at all. Simple obedience brings the right result. Leave the results in God's hands.

> **Galatians 6:9**
> And let us not be weary in well doing: for in due season we shall reap, if we faint not.

Remember Noah.

WINTER

I know many of you can relate to what I'm going to say. The last few years have been the worst and the best. The best because I grew in understanding of the love of God. The worst because I had to go through a lot of heartache to get there. But… God is so faithful. He will use everything in our lives for our good and His glory.

Many of you have heard that some friends are for a lifetime, some for a season, and some for a reason. The last few years, I've learned that I sure didn't have that one figured out in my own life. God knows who we need and when we need them. God is Sovereign and knows what will cause us to grow into the image of His Son. Sometimes it's a very painful process and sometimes it's joyful. It all comes together, for our good and His glory.

When I think of the friends for a season, I'm reminded of someone I heard talk especially about the winter season in our lives. I heard a great man talk about being thankful for the cold spiritual winters we have to endure. It is during the winter that the bugs that damage our crops and parasites that drain the life from the living forms are killed. That helped me apply this to my life. It's during those times that the flowers or "friends" in our lives are proven: "annuals" die and "perennials" endure. The "annuals" are for the "season" and for a "reason". The "perennials" are for a lifetime.

Now, we still need to water and weed the perennials, but they aren't as much work as annuals. That's just like God to give us some special relationships for a lifetime, for which we don't have to work so hard. Those are special blessings.

Thank God for those winter seasons in our lives. Things happen then, and only then, that don't happen any other time in our lives. The parasites lose their grip on our lives and drop out and off. The bugs that destroy our crops are frozen to death with their offspring. It's an okay thing to be in the winter season when you can look at it this way. It's a way for purging, healing, strengthening and rest to occur.

The reason and season friends have served their purpose in your life. They have hopefully helped conform you to the image of the Son. The time you shared life, hopefully, built in you the character of Christ and *vice versa*. You were also in their life for a season and hopefully it accomplished what God intended.

The loss of a friend may cause heartache for a season, but God will heal you. It does take time for some people. There are other relationships that end where we don't grieve at all. We are relieved. Sometimes we remain stupefied by the relationship and outcome, but sooner or later, God will show us the reason.

God will bring more people into your life to build His character in you. Seasons come and go and come around again. Keep your eyes on Him, not the people or the circumstances. We are seasonal friends as well to others. So, let God use your very best to touch their lives. Make a difference whoever you come in contact with for God's glory.

It may be lonely at times, but it is a necessary season set aside to rest from our labors and rest in Him, a season to increase communication with Him. A season of preparation for the spring season of tilling the garden and planting the seed. The winter season is the time to let Him heal us, to get direction from Him, to get instruction from Him, to let Him prune us, to be strengthened, and to rest from labor a while. It all takes time.

Enjoy that winter blast. It has purpose. You have purpose.

FRUIT

Just because a tree in the orchard isn't bearing fruit, that doesn't mean it's not part of the orchard. It could mean the tree hasn't been planted long enough for the roots to grow deep enough to bring nourishment to the branches to bear fruit. It could be it was just transplanted from another orchard, a greenhouse, or maybe a tree nursery. We have to be patient with these trees. We may not see the fruit for a while. But, they're still part of the orchard.

When the tree is big and older and not bearing fruit, something is wrong and needs to be investigated by those in charge of the orchard. There could be damage to the roots. There may not be enough sunlight. There may not be enough water. There may need to be some fertilizer for the roots. There could be something blocking the growth underground. There could be things that need to be removed from the ground and from the branches. A good pruning helps new life to come to the branches many times, but isn't always the only problem. The one in charge of the orchard has to assign someone to prune the branches and fertilize. There may be interference underground, blocking the nourishment to the trees. Investigating that and removing the blockage is not an easy job.

We are of the same orchard. We are the Body of Christ. We need to be patient with each other in our growth and fruit-bearing. Just because someone isn't bearing fruit right now, doesn't mean they aren't part of us. Just because someone isn't growing as tall or strong at the same rate, doesn't mean they aren't part of us. It's a process for everyone and some need more light, or more fertilizer, or more water, or more pruning. We can't see the damaged or blocked roots.

Just like the trees in the orchard, we don't know if someone right next to us is getting the right nourishment they may need from the Word, or prayer, or from fellowship. We don't know whether they are getting enough Sonshine. They may not be spending enough time in God's presence to flourish as they should. We just know something is wrong.

We need to pray. Only the Holy Spirit knows exactly what is causing the growth problem. We need to ask for discernment and wisdom in how we can help. AND, sometimes all we are to do is PRAY. We have to stop trying to fix things for people. Let God have His Hand in it all the way and stay out of His way.

As part of the orchard, we need to share our Sonshine by way of God's love, mercy and grace. We need to share our water by means of encouragement through the Word. We need to help fertilize even when fertilizer isn't wanted. I believe that's called reproof, correction and instruction in righteousness, all the time being led of the Holy Spirit. We can and should all do that. We need to encourage each other daily in the Lord, bringing Sonshine on to each others' lives.

> **Timothy 3:16**
> All Scripture is given by the inspiration of God and is profitable for doctrine, for reproof, for correction, for instruction in righteousness.

> **Hebrew 3:13**
> But exhort one another daily, while it is called today; lest any of you be hardened through the deceitfulness of sin.

God's Word is powerful and sharper than any two-edged sword.

> **Hebrews 4:12**
> For the word of God *is* quick, and powerful, and sharper than any two-edged sword, piercing even to the dividing asunder of soul and spirit, and of the joints and marrow, and *is* a discerner of the thoughts and intents of the heart.

His Word can do so much to free the bound roots and allow proper growth once again.

We need to be instant in season and out of season, with His Word, again fertilizing when led by the Spirit of God.

> **Timothy 4:2**
> Preach the word; be instant in season, out of season; reprove, rebuke, exhort with all longsuffering and doctrine.

As another tree in the orchard, I can share my water. As another tree in the orchard, I can move my branches to let more sunlight in to another. I can even share my fertilizer, but, there are some things another tree can't do.

The One in charge of the orchard has to handle certain things. He's the Only One that can dig deep at the roots and remove what is causing the stunted growth. Another tree can't do that. He's the Only One that can dig below and find what damage may have been done to the root. Another tree can't do that. He's the Only One that can prune the branches so fresh growth can occur with fruit to follow. Another tree can't do that. Some things we have to leave in God's Hands.

God has given us all gifts to use for His Kingdom purposes. We all have our place and assignments. Certain assignments He gives to specific helpers for some of the deeper things. To certain of His Body He has given greater discernment, knowledge, and wisdom to handle difficult root and growth issues. To others, we are assigned to PRAY. Both assignments are of equal value. It's about obedience to the assignment.

Be led of the Spirit of God. Love endures all things. Love is patient and kind.

ROOTS

We've all heard that for a tree to be strong and sturdy and stand against the elements, the roots have to be deep and strong. The roots have to get nourishment from the soil, the water, and the sunshine. We've heard this many times in parallel to our walk with the Lord. So, when they tore up my driveway to repave it because of a tree root problem, I observed some things I will relate to you about tree roots and strength for this life we now live.

The reason I was getting a new driveway was because the roots of this old fir tree continued to grow and literally raised tons of concrete about six inches in some areas. It didn't happen overnight. The roots continued to grow stronger and wider and deeper over time. The roots finally broke up all that heavy weight of the concrete and ended up cracking the whole driveway in many smaller sections and in all directions. Every bit of the driveway was eventually affected by these overgrown roots.

Now, the big root itself that started all the trouble didn't reach all the way through the driveway, but it caused enough destruction in its location, that it affected the whole structure of the driveway in one way or another. The concrete became angled in the wrong direction and couldn't bear up under certain pressure. Because the one large root grew so big and strong, the concrete around it was broken up without much effort at a point of pressure that otherwise wouldn't have affected its strength and integrity.

So, after contemplating this scenario, I came up with some very pertinent things from the Word of God that apply to our lives.

There are two sides to this scenario. We can look at the root as being a hindrance to progress or as health and strength. I'm going to share a little of both.

As we grow stronger in the Word, we will be "rooted and grounded" in this life. Here the big roots are a good thing.

> **Ephesians 3:17**
> That Christ may dwell in your hearts by faith; that ye, being rooted and grounded in love, may be able to comprehend with all saints what is the breadth, and length, and depth, and height; And to know the love of Christ, which passes knowledge, that ye might be filled with all the fullness of God.

The operative Word here is LOVE. Without love, everything else will come to naught.

> **1 Corinthians 13:1-3**
> **1** Though I speak with the tongues of men and of angels, and have not love, I am become *as* sounding brass, or a tinkling cymbal. **2** And though I have *the gift of* prophecy, and understand all mysteries, and all knowledge; and though I have all faith, so that I could remove mountains, and have not love, I am nothing. **3** And though I bestow all my goods to feed *the poor*, and though I give my body to be burned, and have not love, it profiteth me nothing.

> **1 Corinthians 13:13**
> And now abideth faith, hope, love, these three; but the greatest of these *is* love.

> **1 Peter 4:8**
> And above all things have fervent love among yourselves: for love shall cover the multitude of sins.

1 Peter 1:22
Seeing ye have purified your souls in obeying the truth through the Spirit unto unfeigned love of the brethren, *see that ye* love one another with a pure heart fervently:

And, as the Apostle Paul said, "none of these things move me". All the heavy concrete and resulting debris in the driveway didn't stop that root from growing.

Acts 20:24
But none of these things move me, neither count I my life dear unto myself, so that I might finish my course with joy, and the ministry, which I have received of the Lord Jesus, to testify the gospel of the grace of God.

As I was praying one night, I had a vision of what that meant for me: none of these things move me. I was in the middle of a beautiful park. There were several people in the park trying to find refuge from a storm. There was a lot of debris flying around as if in a whirlwind. I was a bronze statue up on a concrete pedestal holding my head up high and arms out. The debris flew around me and hit me constantly, but nothing moved me. Nothing affected me. Nothing hurt me. Nothing wounded me. None of these things moved me at all. I was fixed and steady and stable. The storms will come, but we will stand strong because our roots are strong.

Because the roots are strong and continue to grow, they will remove "those weights that so easily beset us". The concrete of the driveway prevented the full potential of the tree. The weight of the concrete had to go if it was to be the big tree it was meant to be.

Hebrews 12:1-2
Wherefore seeing we also are compassed about with so great a cloud of witnesses, **let us lay aside every weight, and the sin which doth so easily beset *us*,** and let us run with patience the race that is set before us, Looking unto Jesus the author and finisher of *our* faith; who for the joy that was set before him endured the

cross, despising the shame, and is set down at the right hand of the throne of God.

It will take some time, but those pressing and weighty things in our lives can be broken by our strong roots... the power of His Word and the power of the Holy Spirit... the sap, the life-giving nourishment that is operating in our lives. We are told to "break up that fallow ground" in our lives.

> **Hosea 10:12**
> Sow to yourselves in righteousness, reap in mercy; break up your fallow ground: for *it is* time to seek the LORD, till he come and rain righteousness upon you.

> **Jeremiah 4:3**
> For thus saith the LORD to the men of Judah and Jerusalem, Break up your fallow ground, and sow not among thorns.

At the area of the large root growth, there was much resistance and weight. Once the root broke through that resistance, the other areas were more easily broken up around it. That weight had to be removed to get the other areas broken up as well. Just like the concrete breaking easier under pressure because it was at a different angle now, so will the things in our life break up easier, because they are seen at a different angle or perspective. With that growth, we are stronger, and the job of breaking up other areas gets easier. We gain momentum or, you could call it maturity.

Just as we have looked at the positive side of breaking up that concrete by the root, let's look at the opposite side of this. Let's see this big root as the problem. This root may be bitterness, resentment, anger, woundedness, suffering, rejection, abandonment. We could give it a thousand different names. That negative root continues to grow, because it's getting fed. It is feeding on other negative words and negative emotions. It will finally be able to break through whatever was covering it and will show itself strong. What was covering it was probably someone's protection or someone's love. Or, it was covered by hiding, which is the most prominent situation. We, in this human race, hide behind so many things to cover ourselves. Adam and Eve started that for us, covering our shame.

It will most assuredly affect everything and everybody around it. This large, strong root has long range effect. Nearest the large root, the pieces are very broken. The effect of the brokenness is seen far away to the edges where even the larger pieces have at least some cracks, making things unstable there as well.

That's how these negative roots affect our lives and those around us. We may be able to hide some anger, resentment, wounds for a while, but when they are fed and not dealt with, they will cause damage to us and those around us. They will change many things. They will change relationships, opportunities, lifestyle. They may change your destiny.

Jesus wants us to come to Him.

> **Matthew 11:28**
> Come unto me, all you that labor and are heavy laden, and I will give you rest.
>
> **Psalm 142:2** gives us a great starting point, "I poured out my complaint before him; I shewed before him my trouble". He tells us to "pour our complaint out" before Him. Tell Him how you feel about things.

Reading this whole Psalm 142 and Psalm 143 together out loud will help set you free. Let it be your prayer. When it says enemy or trouble, name it. Name the trouble and the problem in your life. Ask the Holy Spirit to help you give it a name. Allow Him to tear up those roots and get them out of your life so that they won't cause anymore problems to you and those around you. Let Him clean you out. Let Him search your heart. Give Him time. Spend time with Him, letting Him speak to you.

Psalm 142
1 I cried unto the LORD with my voice; with my voice unto the LORD did I make my supplication. ² I poured out my complaint before him; I shewed before him my trouble. ³ When my spirit was overwhelmed within me, then thou knewest my path. In the way wherein I walked have they privily laid a snare for me. ⁴ I looked on my right hand, and beheld, but there was no man that would know me: refuge failed me; no man cared for my soul. ⁵ I cried unto thee, O LORD: I said, Thou art my refuge and my portion in the land of the living. ⁶ Attend unto my cry; for I am brought very low: deliver me from my persecutors; for they are stronger than I. ⁷ Bring my soul out of prison, that I may praise thy name: the righteous shall compass me about; for thou shalt deal bountifully with me.

Psalm 143
1Hear my prayer, O LORD, give ear to my supplications: in thy faithfulness answer me, and in thy righteousness. ²And enter not into judgment with thy servant: for in thy sight shall no man living be justified. ³For the enemy hath persecuted my soul; he hath smitten my life down to the ground; he hath made me to dwell in darkness, as those that have been long dead. ⁴Therefore is my spirit overwhelmed within me; my heart within me is desolate. ⁵I remember the days of old; I meditate on all thy works; I muse on the work of thy hands. ⁶I stretch forth my hands unto thee: my soul thirsteth after thee, as a thirsty land. Selah. ⁷Hear me speedily, O LORD: my spirit faileth: hide not thy face from me, lest I be like unto them that go down into the pit. ⁸Cause me to hear thy lovingkindness in the morning; for in thee do I trust: cause me to know the way wherein I should walk; for I lift up my soul unto thee. ⁹Deliver me, O LORD, from mine enemies: I flee unto thee to hide me. ¹⁰Teach me to do thy will; for thou art my God: thy spirit is good; lead me into the land of uprightness. ¹¹Quicken me, O LORD, for thy name's sake: for thy righteousness' sake bring my soul out of trouble.¹²And of thy mercy cut off mine

enemies, and destroy all them that afflict my soul: for I am thy servant.

And, just like the new driveway, "all things become new".

2 Corinthians 5:17
Therefore if any man *be* in Christ, *he is* a new creature: old things are passed away; behold, all things are become new.

Remember, it's a process of becoming.

WHAT ARE YOU LISTENING TO?

What are you listening to? Critical self-evaluation. Our Enemy's accusation. Other's critical speculation. God's Word about our justification.

There should only be one of these we listen to and only one of these things with which we should agree.

God said He is the One to measure. His Word is our measuring stick.

> **2 Corinthians 10:12-13**
> For we dare not make ourselves of the number, or compare ourselves with some that commend themselves: but they measuring themselves by themselves, and comparing themselves among themselves, are not wise. But we will not boast of things without *our* measure, but **according to the measure of the rule which God hath distributed to us**, a measure to reach even unto you.

God said we are justified by faith through His Son, Jesus Christ.

> **Galatians 2:16**
> Knowing that a man is not justified by the works of the law, but **by the faith of Jesus Christ**, even we have believed in Jesus Christ, that we might be **justified by the faith of Christ**, and not by the works of the law: for by the works of the law shall no flesh be justified.
>
> **Romans 5:1** Therefore being **justified by faith**, we have peace with God **through our Lord Jesus Christ:** 2 By

whom also we have access by faith into this grace wherein we stand, and rejoice in hope of the glory of God.

God said our sins are covered.

> **Romans 4:7**
> *Saying,* Blessed *are* they whose iniquities are forgiven, and whose **sins are covered**.

God said we are His kids.

> **Galatians 3:26**
> For ye are all **the children of God** by faith in Christ Jesus.

God said we are a royal priesthood.

> **1 Peter 2:9**
> But ye *are* a chosen generation, a **royal priesthood**, an holy nation, a peculiar people; that ye should shew forth the praises of him who hath called you out of darkness into his marvelous light:

God said we are His workmanship.

> **Ephesians 2:10**
> For **we are his workmanship**, created in Christ Jesus unto good works, which God hath before ordained that we should walk in them.

God said He has a plan, a future, and a hope for us.

> **Jeremiah 29:11**
> For I know the thoughts that I think toward you, saith the LORD, thoughts of peace, and not of evil, **to give you an expected end**.

God said we are more than conquerors.

Romans 8:37
Nay, in all these things we are **more than conquerors** through him that loved us.

God said we can come boldly to His Throne of Grace. Oh yeah! GRACE!!!

Hebrew 4:16
Let us therefore come boldly unto the throne of grace, that we may obtain mercy, and find grace to help in time of need.

These are some things we forget to tell ourselves in our own evaluation. These are some of the Scriptures we need to keep ever before us to remind ourselves of His Words about us. These are some things that others forget to mention in their speculation about us. These are some things that the enemy doesn't include in his accusations about us. God's GRACE… greater than all our sin!

Romans 5:20
But where sin abounded, grace did much more abound:

It's not about deserving His grace. It's His gift just because He loves us. You can't earn it. His grace just abounds, whether we believe it or not, His grace abounds toward us.

2 Corinthians 4:15
For all things *are* for your sakes, that the abundant grace might through the thanksgiving of many redound to the glory of God.

James 4:6
But he giveth more grace. Wherefore he saith, God resisteth the proud, but giveth grace unto the humble.

We have to stop beating ourselves up. We have to stop wasting time. We have to stop walking in agreement with our Enemy. We have to stop thinking on critical self-evaluation. We have to stop

On To The Prize

thinking about our enemy's accusations. We have to stop thinking about others' speculation. We need to start thinking about what God says about our justification.

> **Proverbs 23:7**
> As a man thinks in his heart, so is he.
>
> **Philippians 4:8**
> Finally, brethren, whatsoever things are true, whatsoever things *are* honest, whatsoever things *are* just, whatsoever things *are* pure, whatsoever things *are* lovely, whatsoever things *are* of good report; if *there be* any virtue, and if *there be* any praise, think on these things.

So think on whatsoever things that are pure Word, honestly allowing the Holy Spirit to search our heart. Think on our justification through our Savior Jesus Christ, and of the good report of God's grace and love beyond measure. And, not only think on these things, but speak these things to yourself regularly. Speaking and hearing build our faith and makes us stronger.

Think on His Word. Speak His Word. Listen to His Word.

THE SHED

I was cleaning out my shed to reorganize, scale down, and get ready to move other things in for storage before winter. When I was compacting things, I had to organize tightly and to the ceiling. There were a few items that couldn't stand alone, or fit in some places because they were made of weaker material or of an unstable structure that couldn't tolerate the pressure of something heavier on top of it or against it. Some things were not in a convenient shape to store in a very organized fashion as some of the other items. When I found little open areas, I was able to put certain items into the gaps, and they were then supported by the other things that were stronger. The weaker or unstable items were then being able to stand up without leaning or falling.

The main thought: This is a picture of the Church. We are supposed to be so close together that we support each other no matter what shape we're in. There is no way the one that is weaker or of an inconvenient shape should fall. If they are closely supported by all those around, they will not fall.

I've heard many times in my life in the Church and have said it myself: "I just don't fit in". What are their expectations? What are your expectations? It should be what the Word of God expects from us, not what we expect from others or ourselves. Here's how all of us fit into the Church.

> **1 Thessalonians 5: 11-14** gives us a good picture of what the New Testament Church, the Body of Christ, should act like:
>
> **11 Wherefore comfort yourselves together, and edify one another, even as also ye do. 12** And we beseech you, brethren, to know them which labour among you, and are over you in the Lord, and admonish you; **13** And to **esteem them very highly in love** for their work's sake. *And* **be at peace among yourselves. 14** Now we exhort you, brethren, **warn them that are unruly, comfort the feebleminded, support the weak, be patient toward all** *men.*

The Scripture very clearly states we are to support the weak, edify and comfort one another, live in peace with one another, and esteem those in authority with love.

Hebrews 3:13 tells us **why** we should act like the Church in Thessalonica was instructed.

> But exhort one another daily, while it is called To day; lest any of you be hardened through the deceitfulness of sin.

We should encourage, strengthen, build up, acknowledge, appreciate, respect, warn and be patient. We are to support one another every day. Why do we do those things? That no one will become hardened by sin, and that they would remain steadfast and strong.

All these things aren't easy to do, but practice makes perfect. Practice patience, kindness, exhortation, acknowledgment, appreciation, and respect. Practice the Word of God when we are told to go to a brother.

> **Galatians 6:1**
> Brethren, if a man be overtaken in a fault, ye which are spiritual, restore such an one in the spirit of meekness; considering thyself, lest thou also be tempted.
>
> **Matthew 5:24-25**
> **24** Therefore if thou bring thy gift to the altar, and there rememberest that thy brother hath ought against thee; **25** Leave there thy gift before the altar, and go thy way; first be reconciled to thy brother, and then come and offer thy gift.

We all fit into the Church. We all fit into the Body of Christ. Even when we feel like a square peg in a round hole, there is always something we can do for the Body. We simply obey the Word: encourage, exhort, strengthen, acknowledge, appreciate, respect, warn, be patient.

Please notice that in the description of what the Church should be, it's all about someone else. It's not about me. It's about others. It's about what I can do to help others. It's about what I can do to bless someone else. It's what I can do to take care of someone else. It's about helping someone else stand up. It's about supporting others. Too many are focused on their own circumstances and own life;but God promises that if we seek Him first, He will take care of it all.

> **Matthew 6:33**
> But seek ye first the kingdom of God, and his righteousness; and all these things shall be added unto you.

Let's practice seeking Him first and blessing the Body of Christ. We will see great and mighty things we have never seen before begin to happen in our lives and those we love.

Support your brothers and sisters.

CLOUDS

Flying above the clouds they look like big cotton balls. Looks like you could just jump into them and be enveloped by the softness. Of course, we know that that is just what it "looks like". The consequences of trying that jump into the clouds is completely different than what would be expected from what it "looks like".

How many times have our eyes not been wide open, and we jumped into something not expecting the results we got? How many times have we gone into a situation that looked one way, yet turned out to be something completely different? Everything isn't always as it appears. We've all walked into something or feel like we've gotten trapped into something at one time or another that didn't appear as it actually was.

There are always consequences for poor choices and poor judgment calls. That's why it is so important that our spiritual eyes are opened to all that goes on around us. Having our spiritual eyes open is so very important to avoid unnecessary consequences for our actions and delays in our progress in our walk with God. We don't want to waste our time going into situations that will detour us from the direction God has planned for our life.

Those spiritual eyes have a name; it's called discernment. Discernment comes to us in a few different ways.

It is a gift from God.

> **1 Corinthians 12:1-12**
> Now concerning spiritual gifts, brethren, I would not have you ignorant. ² Ye know that ye were Gentiles, carried away unto these dumb idols, even as ye were led. ³ Wherefore I give you to understand, that no man speaking by the Spirit of God calleth Jesus accursed: and that no man can say that Jesus is the Lord, but by the Holy Ghost. ⁴ Now there are diversities of gifts, but the same Spirit. ⁵ And there are differences of administrations, but the same Lord. ⁶ And there are diversities of operations, but it is the same God which worketh all in all. ⁷ But the manifestation of the Spirit is given to every man to profit withal. ⁸ For to one is given by the Spirit the word of wisdom; to another the word of knowledge by the same Spirit; ⁹ To another faith by the same Spirit; to another the gifts of healing by the same Spirit; ¹⁰ To another the working of miracles; to another prophecy; to another ***discerning of spirits;*** to another divers kinds of tongues; to another the interpretation of tongues: ¹¹ But all these worketh that one and the selfsame Spirit, dividing to every man severally as he will. ¹² For as the body is one, and hath many members, and all the members of that one body, being many, are one body: so also is Christ.

The Holy Spirit gives these gifts to those who need it. He gives as He wills. He gives as we need them. We have to be open to receive what we need for ministry to others and to function how God planned for us to function in the Kingdom of God on this earth.

It comes with experience.

> **Romans 5:3**
> And not only so, but we glory in tribulations also: knowing that *tribulation worketh patience;* ⁴ *And patience, experience; and experience, hope.* ⁵ And hope maketh not ashamed; because the love of God is shed abroad in our hearts by the Holy Ghost which is given unto us.

All the things we go through hopefully work patience in us, and through them, we gather experience and understanding. As we understand more we discern more. We have hope in God through our trials, tests, and tribulations because we have experienced His Hand in our lives time and time again. We know from experience that God will come through for us.

It comes by practice.

> **Hebrews 5:13-14**
> For every one that useth milk is unskillful in the word of righteousness: for he is a babe. [14] But strong meat belongeth to them that are of full age, even *those who by reason of use have their senses exercised to discern both good and evil.*

Here the writer of Hebrews is talking about the use of the Word of God. The "strong meat" of the Word is for the more mature and experienced. As they are studying and hearing and living the Word, their senses are more discerning to both good and evil.

It comes by praying for wisdom.

> **Proverbs 4:7**
> Wisdom is the principal thing; therefore get wisdom: and with all thy getting get understanding.

> **James 1:5**
> *If any of you lack wisdom, let him ask of God,* that giveth to all men liberally, and upbraideth not; and it shall be given him.

Through asking for wisdom, time and time again, we become experienced in hearing God, we are practicing His Word, and thereby, increasing in discernment. We get understanding, which is discernment.

Proverbs 2:2
So that thou incline thine ear unto wisdom, and apply thine heart to understanding;

Proverbs 19:8
He that getteth wisdom loveth his own soul: he that keepeth understanding shall find good.

Proverbs 3:13
Happy is the man that findeth wisdom, and the man that getteth understanding.

We need discernment so we can guard our hearts against attacks of the enemy. We need discernment so we can avoid bad situations. In this age in which we live, our enemy is working overtime to distract and discourage. We need discernment to avoid those pitfalls. We need discernment to stop the delay in our progress in the Kingdom of God.

Deuteronomy 4:8-10
And what nation is there so great, that hath statutes and judgments so righteous as all this law, which I set before you this day? [9] Only take heed to thyself, and keep thy soul diligently, lest thou forget the things which thine eyes have seen, and lest they depart from thy heart all the days of thy life: but teach them thy sons, and thy sons' sons; [10] Specially the day that thou stoodest before the LORD thy God in Horeb, when the LORD said unto me, Gather me the people together, and I will make them hear my words, that they may learn to fear me all the days that they shall live upon the earth, and that they may teach their children.

Get our heads out of the clouds and get discernment.

BLACK TOP

One day I was driving, and I thought that this sure was a bumpy road to have fresh black top. I saw some of the road workers filling in some holes ahead of the black top machine. My thinking at that point was that they were doing a quick and easy way of repair. It didn't appear they were laying down a firm enough understructure in the potholes and a thick enough layer of black top. But, hey, I'm just an observer. So, sure enough, it wasn't a year later, and they were at it again. This time, they did it right.

To get new black top put down on a road, there are several things that have to happen. There first have to be complaints that something is wrong with the integrity of the road. The condition of the road is causing damage to cars and is unsafe for driving because of the many potholes, lumps, and bumps. The road commission has their own people always on the lookout for road damage, but they need the observations of the John Q. Public to help them as well. Can't leave everything to the professionals.

People will put up with the rough ride for a while, but as more and more complaints pour into the officials in charge, something has to be done. Sometimes people will just start taking another route instead of putting up with the rough ride. Some drivers will take another route because they are tired of waiting for someone to do something about the damage. They don't want to have damage to their vehicles or even get hurt because of consistently taking that road of disrepair.

The officials have to actually see the damage themselves before they will do something about it. The road commission will then investigate all areas that are in disrepair for that particular stretch of road. They want to know what they are dealing with before they invest time and money into such a project. It may even take something drastic to happen to get things moving along.

Sometimes the area can be fixed without laying down all new road, but many times, because of the wear and tear, several areas need repair at the same time. They have to lay a good foundation before they can put down the new layer of black top. So, these areas have to be fixed with many layers of support sometimes before the new black top can be applied. Without that layered, stable foundation, what looked so nice at first will erode rather quickly from the continued use and weight of traffic.

I know, some of you may be thinking, where is she going with all this? So many things pop into my heart and mind on this subject. Some of you are there already. You already know where this is going. Having a word picture many times helps us draw strong truths from God's Word about our walk with God and our life in the Body of Christ.

I first want to talk about the leadership in the Body of Christ. Those in charge of leading the Sheep should have our best interest at heart and be ready to help find those areas of disrepair. Leadership in charge of ministry to the Body of Christ should be always on the lookout for the areas needing repair. They should be keeping a watchful eye on things that need to have a firmer foundation to build on.

And, did you notice that "they" investigate? This speaks to me of the ministry of the leadership in the Body of Christ. "They". This speaks to me of the wisdom and safety we find in a multitude of counselors.

Proverbs 11:14
Where no counsel *is*, the people fall: but in the multitude of counselors *there is* safety.
Proverbs 15:22
Without counsel purposes are disappointed: but in the multitude of counselors they are established.

Proverbs 24:6
For by wise counsel thou shalt make thy war: and in multitude of counselors *there is* safety.

"They" evaluate, investigate, and do something about it. This speaks to me of the work of the Holy Spirit in our lives. The road commission wants to make sure the road is stable before they invest all the money and time needed to put down the new black top. What if there was a sinkhole? Black top sure wouldn't do the trick there. A firmer foundation has to be laid.

Sounds just like us. We want to do so much for the Lord and work in the Kingdom of God, but we keep getting hung up. It seems we take one step forward and two steps backward. Many times we want the quick fix for our issues by covering them up and burying them so no one can see them. We don't want to let the Holy Spirit heal us or the Body of Christ help us heal. We don't want to get wisdom and counsel because it would reveal our "disrepair". We are content many times to go on with the familiar so no attention is drawn to the disrepair.

We sometimes start taking a different route to deal with the disrepair. This may mean changing friends, changing churches, changing jobs, changing habits, changing relationships. Anything that takes the discomfort away so we don't have to deal with the "disrepair", we find a way.

The Bible tells us in Psalm 142:2 to "pour our complaint out before the Lord". Let Him know what you are going through and how you feel. He already knows. But He tells us in Matthew and Luke to keep asking, keep knocking, keep seeking.

> **Luke 11:9**
> And I say unto you, Ask, and it shall be given you; seek, and ye shall find; knock, and it shall be opened unto you.

Don't take another route to comfort. Don't take another route to avoid feeling your feelings, and feeling your pain. Don't take another route to avoid facing the things in life that have to be changed. When that road gets bumpy and needs repair, let the Holy Spirit do His work in you.

We all have areas that need repair. Sometimes we haven't allowed the Holy Spirit to heal us because it may be too deep and wide… too painful. Or, it may be pride in the way of asking for help. James 5:16 states: "Confess your faults (sins, hurts, etc.) one to another, and pray one for another, that ye may be healed". Healing comes through confessing and then praying for each other.

God wants to do many new things in our lives. He wants to do abundantly above all that we could ever ask or think (Ephesians 3:20). We may have learned more, grown deeper in our walk with the Lord, been used in a new area of ministry, but if we don't allow the Holy Spirit to heal us, it won't be long before we're looking just like we did before. The same issues keep coming up and up and up.

Those "weights" that so easily beset us will cause the disrepair to show through again and again. Let the Holy Spirit dig deep to heal those areas of woundedness so you will have a firm foundation for God to build you up for His Kingdom purposes and glory.

> **Hebrews 12:1**
> Wherefore seeing we also are compassed about with so great a cloud of witnesses, let us lay aside every weight, and the sin which doth so easily beset us, and let us run with patience the race that is set before us.

Build up your foundation. Let God repair and restore.

TASTEFULNESS

There have been four basic tastes: sweet, sour, bitter, salty. But, as of the last few years, the experts have decided there is also "savory". In the right combination, there can be great flavor. In the wrong combination, there can be very bad flavor.

Taste depends on the taste buds of the taster. There are tastes that are more pleasing to some than others because of exposure to certain flavors while growing up. Some tastes are definitely acquired through repetition. What one thinks palatable, another may not. Where there has been damage to taste buds, things taste differently. So, no matter what seasoning you use, these taste buds won't taste many things as intended.

Haven't we all experienced that in our communication with people? No matter what you say or do for some people, they can't "taste" your words or gestures in the way you intended? What you think is palatable, they may not? You haven't been exposed to things they have been exposed to, and vice versa, so you don't "taste" things the same way. Therefore, misunderstandings occur.

We may look at the bitter, sour, salty, sweet, and savory taste buds as personality or character flaws or we could look at them as conditions of the soul. In our communication with others, it may be "no taste", which is so much damage they can't receive anything as intended. Or it may be "sour taste" or "bitter taste" or "savory taste" or "sweet taste" or "salty taste" that overpowers the "real" taste. The "real" taste is sometimes pleasant and sometimes unpleasant. Some people may want to sweeten things up when it's unpleasant and decide not to experience the "real" taste. Some may want to not taste it at all.

Sometimes we have "tasted" so many unpleasant things in life, we are sick and tired of trying. Certain situations in our lives may have left such a bad taste in our spiritual and emotional mouths that we won't even give it a try anymore. We refuse to open up and even "taste and see" that the Lord is good. He wants to be in every area of our lives.

> **Psalm 34:8**
> O taste and see that the LORD *is* good: blessed *is* the man *that* trusteth in him.

When something isn't received in the way we intended it, remember that person's "taste buds" have been damaged. When we don't receive things the way another person intended, we have to look within ourselves as well for damage control.

> **Psalm 139:23-24**
> Search me, O God, and know my heart: try me, and know my thoughts: And see if *there be any* wicked way in me, and lead me in the way everlasting.

In our communication with people, it usually doesn't take long to see damage has happened somewhere along the way. So we have to "flavor" our words a little differently to communicate with each person. But Christ already told us we should do that.

> **Colossians 4:6**.
> Let your speech be always with grace, seasoned with salt, that ye may know how ye ought to answer every man.

Communicating is a must in the Kingdom of God. Doing good and communicating are sacrifices that please God. He tells us it is very important, so no matter how difficult it may seem, we must please the Father. The Holy Spirit is there to guide us and give us the answers and the words to speak.

Hebrews 13:16
But to do good and to communicate forget not: for with such sacrifices God is well pleased.

Luke 21:14-15
Settle *it* therefore in your hearts, not to meditate before what ye shall answer: For I will give you a mouth and wisdom, which all your adversaries shall not be able to gainsay nor resist.

It appears that "salt" is a very important flavor in every combination. If you are a baker, you know that in every recipe for baked-goods, there is salt. Salt brings out the flavor in every kind of food. You don't need a lot of it either. So, in combination with every other herb, spice, and flavor, salt will bring out the best flavor.

Mark 9:50
Salt *is* good: but if the salt have lost his saltness, wherewith will ye season it? Have salt in yourselves, and have peace one with another.

No matter what is going on with a person, bitter or sour, or always serious, which I call savory, we are the salt of the earth and here to savor it.

Let our speech be seasoned with grace and love.

LOVESICK

Have you ever been around a person who was lovesick? They are giddy and all they can talk about is their love. No matter what subject matter you get on, they slip in something about what their love thinks or says about it too. Or, they may lose track of what you are talking about, because they are thinking of their love. Instead of engaged in conversation with you, they are in lala land, daydreaming.

We all want someone's undivided attention, no matter what's going on around them or in them. But, when someone is lovesick, we cannot keep them off the subject of their love.

The Bible tells in **Romans 12:15**:
> Rejoice with them that do rejoice, and weep with them that weep.

So, despite what we want to communicate about, we need to rejoice with them in their lovesick state.

Now, there are usually two different reactions. Either it makes you "sick" as in disgusted, or it warms your heart to see the joy they are experiencing. Sharing their joy blesses you and excites you for them.

If you have reaction number one, you may have been hurt so badly yourself, that you hate the subject matter. You may have never had the experience, so you don't comprehend the depth of the emotion and love. You may have had the experience, but the feelings of excitement and love have worn off, so you now take your love for granted. Or, you have let all the circumstances of life weigh you down and discourage you to the point of wanting out of this relationship. It becomes too much work. You have become focused on yourself instead of the love of your life.

Then there are those who have reaction number two. That is a person who falls deeper and deeper in love with their love every day. That is a person who loves unconditionally. That is a grateful person. That is a person who appreciates what they have. That is a person who understands how precious love really is. To find someone who loves you no matter what and stays by your side. To find someone who walks through the good, bad and ugly of your life without giving up on you. To find someone who will help you through and lift you up when you fall. To find someone who continually gives of themselves to make sure you are the best you can be… That is a person who understands lovesickness.

When I was thinking about this subject and decided to do my commentary, I knew you would know where I was going with this. But, I think this bears a little investigation for the purpose of our evaluation for a healthy soul.

When we first discover that Jesus loves us, we are so overwhelmed with His mercy, His love, His grace, His patience. The list goes on and on. As we develop our relationship with Him, we grow in our knowledge and understanding. We are lovesick for Him. We hunger and thirst after His righteousness. We are spending our time with Him or talking about Him to others. We can't help ourselves. He's the center of our universe and we are lovesick for Him.

Then, things start happening that we don't understand. Painful events hit us with blow after blow as we walk along in this relationship. Situations begin to overwhelm us. We get our eyes off of Him and onto the circumstances surrounding us. We become self-focused.

The Apostle Paul is one of the strongest examples we can give for someone who experienced afflictions, trials, and tests. He knew this was all a part of this life, but God was in the midst of it all, giving strength and wisdom through it all.

> **2 Corinthians 6:4-10**
> 4 But in all *things* approving ourselves as the ministers of God, in much patience, in afflictions, in necessities, in distresses, 5 In stripes, in imprisonments, in tumults, in labours, in watchings, in fastings; 6 By pureness, by knowledge, by longsuffering, by kindness, by the Holy Ghost, by love unfeigned, 7 By the word of truth, by the power of God, by the armour of righteousness on the right hand and on the left, 8 By honour and dishonour, by evil report and good report: as deceivers, and *yet* true; 9 As unknown, and *yet* well known; as dying, and, behold, we live; as chastened, and not killed; 10 As sorrowful, yet alway rejoicing; as poor, yet making many rich; as having nothing, and *yet* possessing all things.

We begin to question His protection and love for us. Our trust in Him and His ability to protect, love, and guide us wanes. We begin to think we can do things on our own without communication with Him.

> **John 15:5**
> I am the vine; you are the branches. If you remain in me and I in you, you will bear much fruit; **apart from me you can do nothing**.

We soon see that doing things on our own doesn't really work either. Instead of going back to our Lover, we try other avenues of relief to no avail. We look to others to solve problems and give us that same "feeling" we had of peace and joy. Which means, we have transferred our affections to another lover.

We have to remember what His Word tells us. No matter what happens, He is with us and will deliver us from it. We have to spend time with Him and get our eyes off the circumstances.

> **John 16:33**
> These things I have spoken unto you, that in me ye might have peace. In the world ye shall have tribulation: but be of good cheer; I have overcome the world.
>
> **Psalm 34:19**
> Many *are* the afflictions of the righteous: but the LORD delivereth him out of them all.

Some of us wouldn't be able to tolerate what Paul went through, and keep our love intact. This shows us that no matter what, we can be victorious and can keep our first love. We can still remain lovesick for Jesus no matter what comes our way in this life. We can keep Him as the center of our lives and heart. Nothing can separate us from the LOVE. Only our own decisions separate our hearts from His heart.

> **Romans 8:38-39**
> 38 For I am persuaded, that neither death, nor life, nor angels, nor principalities, nor powers, nor things present, nor things to come, 39 Nor height, nor depth, nor any other creature, shall be able to separate us from the love of God, which is in Christ Jesus our Lord.

The Bible tells us that it rains on the just and unjust. Bad things do happen, but that doesn't change God's love for us.

> **Matthew 5:45**
> That ye may be the children of your Father which is in heaven: for he maketh his sun to rise on the evil and on the good, and sendeth rain on the just and on the unjust.

God is lovesick for us. He thinks about us all the time. He rejoices over us with singing. He dances over us. We are the apple of His eye. He waits in expectation for fellowship with us.

> **Zephaniah 3:17**
> The LORD thy God in the midst of thee *is* mighty; he will save, he will rejoice over thee with joy; he will rest in his love, he will joy over thee with singing.

> **Psalm 40:5**
> Many, O LORD my God, *are* thy wonderful works *which* thou hast done, and thy thoughts *which are* to us-ward: they cannot be reckoned up in order unto thee: *if* I would declare and speak *of them*, they are more than can be numbered.

> **Jeremiah 29:11**
> For I know the thoughts that I think toward you, saith the LORD, thoughts of peace, and not of evil, to give you an expected end.

God talks about us leaving our first love. He says we must repent for leaving our first love. He wants us to go back to the place where we first met Him. He wants us to return to the place where we talked about Him all the time and fellowshipped with Him.

> **Revelation 2:4-5**
> Nevertheless I have *somewhat* against thee, because thou hast left thy first love. Remember therefore from whence thou art fallen, and repent, and do the first works; or else I will come unto thee quickly, and will remove thy candlestick out of his place, except thou repent.

I used to sing a song about this very thing years ago. It was called "First Love" by Steve Fry. I can't locate the lyrics on the internet, but do remember one verse that says what needs to be said:

> "Take me back to my first love.
> To the place where I once was.

Where my passion was just obeying.
And prayer was sweet, the sweetest thing I knew
Everything was possible with You
Take me back to the place of my first love with You."

Let these words be a prayer for you if you haven't been lovesick in a while.

I know God, the Lover of our soul, longs to hear this following verse from our lips:

Isaiah 26:8
Yea, in the way of thy judgments, O LORD, have we waited for thee; the desire of *our* soul *is* to thy name, and to the remembrance of thee.

The desire of our soul should be Him, to praise Him, love Him, worship Him, share Him. Thinking of Him should be our joy. Fellowshipping with Him should be our excitement everyday. If we aren't lovesick for the Lover of our Soul, if we aren't acting lovesick for Him, there's a problem.

Be lovesick for Jesus.

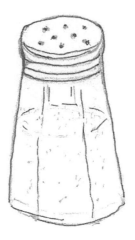

HOW'S YOUR SALT LEVEL?

Mark 9:50
Salt is good: but if the salt have lost his saltness, wherewith will ye season it? Have salt in yourselves, and have peace one with another.

Matthew 5:13
Ye are the salt of the earth: but if the salt have lost his savour, wherewith shall it be salted? It is thenceforth good for nothing, but to be cast out, and to be trodden under foot of men.

Salt can be used in several different ways. I've been thinking about all the different properties of salt and can see spiritual implications in every one of them. And, no matter what the property is, if the salt has lost its "saltness", chemically it will not work in that property. For a lack of a better word to get my point across, I am using the word from the King James Version of the Bible: "saltness". The word "saltness" implies "salty", and, as you will see, that is only one property of salt.

Mark tells us to "have salt in yourselves" …hmmmm. That's an interesting way to put it. In many translations of the Bible, it says the same thing. Then what is salt referring to here? It could be several things. The verse before this one says they will be "salted with fire" (Mark 9:49). So, then salt has to be looked at as a verb, noun, adjective, and adverb. It has to be something that can be poured out. If we are to have salt within us, let's see what the Word says about what should be "in" us that can be poured out. Because salt doesn't do any good if it stays in the container. It must have to be poured out to accomplish its purpose. So, after researching this, I believe we can see in the Word what we are to be filled with so we can pour it back out.

Ephesians 3:19
And to know the love of Christ, which passes knowledge, that ye might be **filled *with all the fullness of God*.**

Ephesians 5:18
And be not drunk with wine, wherein is excess; but be **filled *with the Spirit*,**

Colossians 1:9
For this cause we also, since the day we heard it, do not cease to pray for you, and to desire that ye might be **filled *with the knowledge of His will in all wisdom and spiritual understanding.***

2 Timothy 1:4
Greatly desiring to see thee, being mindful of thy tears, that I may be **filled *with joy.***

So "saltness" must be, in short, being filled with the fullness of God on a continual basis, which means God's character, by the power of the Holy Spirit. The list of the attributes of God is endless, but there are a few attributes that need to be preeminent.

Galatians 5:22-23
But the fruit of the Spirit is love, joy, peace, longsuffering, gentleness, goodness, faith Meekness, temperance: against such there is no law.

We achieve that by being transformed by the renewing of our minds.

> **Romans 12:2**
> And be not conformed to this world: but be ye transformed by the renewing of your mind, that ye may prove what *is* that good, and acceptable, and perfect will of God.

We do this through studying God's Word, meditating on God's Word, listening to God's Word, sharing God's Word, fellowshipping, building up the Body of Christ, praying, praising, thanking, worshiping. The result will be that our joy will be full.

In His presence is fullness of joy, and His joy is my strength, so I must have to be in His presence and fellowship with Him and His Word to keep full, to keep joy and to keep strong. Open your spirit to the Holy Spirit and the Word. Let the Holy Spirit search your heart so you can see your measure of fullness.

In measuring our "saltness" level, let's apply the different properties of salt to our walk with God.

SALT GIVES FLAVOR

Did you know that salting something helps bring out its natural flavor? That's why even a little salt is better than no salt. You know that too much salt can ruin something and the true flavor then can't be tasted.

If you keep "salt" in yourself, your natural flavor will come out. The person God has called you to be will be available to Him and to others. If you get too salty, no one can tolerate you. You have to communicate in this world with real people who are in this worldly system. Don't go overboard. Be real, open, and communicate with flavor.

> **Colossians 4:6**
> Let your speech *be* alway with grace, seasoned with salt, that ye may know how ye ought to answer every man.

If you keep "salting" others, their natural flavor will come out. You will see them through the eyes of Jesus and be able to minister appropriately. If you salt them too much, they will be overwhelmed.

SALT PRESERVES

Did you know that a salty brine helps preserve things for years? That's why something good tasting can be expected even after years of preservation.

If you keep "salt" in yourself, you will have the strength to run the race, strength to endure. After all, this walk with God is an endurance race. We must be preserved to be able to fulfill His purposes for us.

If we "salt" others, we will help preserve them as well. Encouraging each other daily in the Lord is a form of preserving each other, salting each other.

> **1 Thessalonians 5:11**
> Therefore encourage one another and build one another up, just as you are doing.

> **1 Thessalonians 5:14**
> And we urge you, brothers, admonish the idle, encourage the fainthearted, help the weak, be patient with them all.

SALT CAUSES THIRST

Did you know that salt, even in small amounts can cause thirst? Everybody is different. Everybody needs a different amount of salt to become thirsty. Only God knows the level of salt intake a person needs to cause them to thirst. So you may have to keep adding salt. Only those who "hunger and thirst after righteousness will be filled" (Matthew 5:6). Let's help them by salting them.

SALT STOPS ODOR

Did you know that when you are cooking raw meat and get that less than favorable raw meat mixed with blood smell permeating the air, just salt it, and the smell will go away? Jesus tells us to love the unlovely. Those who are the less favorable people to have relationships with are just those that God has called us to "salt".

> **Luke 6:32**
> If you love those who love you, what credit is that to you? For even sinners love those who love them.

> **Matthew 5:44**
> But I say unto you, love your enemies, bless them that curse you, do good to them that hate you, and pray for them which despitefully use you, and persecute you.

Many of us would rather not. But, how then are we different from the world? Salt them!

SALT BURNS

Did you know that salt on delicate skin or on an abrasion or cut can cause burning? The burning sensation doesn't last long. There are also healing properties in that salt that occur even after causing the burn. Again, everybody can tolerate different levels of salt. Be led by the Holy Spirit when using your salt shaker.

SALT IS ABRASIVE

Did you know that salt can be used as a cleansing agent because of its abrasive property? Clean-up in aisle 6!!! Sometimes we are called upon to clean up a mess. There are different assignments for each one of us. And, some have to clean up more messes than others. Ask for God's wisdom. Be obedient to the Holy Spirit.

> **Galatians 6:1**
> Brethren, if a man be overtaken in a fault, ye which are spiritual, restore such a one in the spirit of meekness; considering thyself, lest thou also be tempted.

Remember that "apart from Me, you can do nothing".

> **John 15:5**
> I am the vine, ye *are* the branches: He that abideth in me, and I in him, the same bringeth forth much fruit: for without me ye can do nothing.

He will give you the wisdom to operate your salt shaker.

SALT CAUSES BUOYANCY

Did you know that you can't sink in really salty water? You float. As long as you keep enough salt around and through you, you will not sink! You, however, are the one who has to envelope yourself in the "saltness" of others, and spread the salt around. When you feel like you are sinking in the overwhelming circumstances of life, check the salt level around you. Are you fellowshipping enough? Are you doing Body life?

> **Hebrews 13:3** But exhort one another daily, while it is called today; lest any of you be hardened through the deceitfulness of sin.

Encourage each other in the Lord while it is called today, so no one sinks.

SALT MELTS ICE

Did you know that when you throw salt on ice, it melts? If you aren't a Northerner, you might not know that. It's a process and takes some time, but it works. Did you know there is a temperature at which it is too cold for salt to melt ice? At about 10 degrees, salt will no longer melt ice, but at that point, it can be used for traction. But as the temperature rises, just a little, the salt can then do its best work of melting.

Sometimes melting ice is the only way to someone's heart. God knows who these people are. He knows whose heart is too cold. He knows He can still use your salt for traction in their lives. You can get a footing when standing up against their ice. The salt may need to be applied with these people in one of the other manners previously mentioned. Listen to Him.

IN SUMMARY:

God knows each individual. He knows our hearts. He knows our circumstances. He loves us so much. Only He knows how the salt will be used in our lives. Only He knows what "saltness" we will need. Our purpose is to be "filled" with salt and saltness.

Your job is to keep your salt shaker full and keep salting all those around you.

A PRESSURE WASHER

When I was pressure washing my house, I began to think about why a pressure washer worked so well. Whoever designed them really helped mankind with easier cleanup. I sure was grateful. I just thought of the mechanics of the whole thing and, here to, could apply this to our lives.

The water comes in running full force from the faucet to the end of the regular sized hose. The first part of the attachment for a pressure washer has a smaller diameter tube to build up pressure for the water from the main hose to push through. There is a pressure valve after that tube which releases the built-up pressure through yet another much smaller diameter and longer tube. At that point, there is an external squeeze handle that you can control. When you squeeze the handle, it then can force the water out even at a higher pressure to clean up where you are aiming the spray. But, at the end of the sprayer, you have four different attachments to use. Each one has a different scope, aim, and pressure.

My spirit did a little leap within me when I learned the information about how a pressure washer worked. It is so much like our lives in the Spirit.

John 15:5
I am the vine, ye *are* the branches: He that abideth in me, and I in him, the same bringeth forth much fruit: for without me ye can do nothing.

I thought about how He is communicating with us all the time through the Holy Spirit: Flowing to us and through us. He is the Vine that brings the life juices to the branches so they can bring forth fruit.

The flow can only be turned off at the Source. He, the Vine, is our Source. He is the only One Who can stop the flow of life-giving nutrients. The flow with power can only be released when we squeeze the handle. We have control of that valve. We squeeze the handle and let it flow out. The force and speed at which the Holy Spirit will flow from us we obviously cannot comprehend. God's Spirit (the faucet) is flowing to us (the big hose) and through us at all times.

> **John 7:38**
> He that believeth on me, as the Scripture hath said, out of his belly shall flow rivers of living water.

He says that we should have springs of Living Water within our souls that should flood out of us over all those around us. Out of us should flow life, and life abundantly.

We have control of that valve. Are we letting the cares of this world keep that valve shut? Are we letting the pride of life keep that valve shut? We need to open that valve to the Holy Spirit everyday so we can affect everyone and everything we come in contact with. It's about His power flowing through us. It's about us opening that valve to let His power flow. We are responsible for affecting those around us. Let the River flow.

I thought about our narrow path and how much narrower it seems to be getting as time marches on to the Prize that is set before us and the glory that awaits us.

> **Matthew 7:13, 14**
> Enter ye in at the strait gate: for wide *is* the gate, and broad *is* the way, that leadeth to destruction, and many

there be which go in thereat: Because strait *is* the gate, and **narrow *is* the way, which leadeth unto life,** and few there be that find it.

Hebrews 12:1-2
Wherefore seeing we also are compassed about with so great a cloud of witnesses, let us lay aside every weight, and the sin which doth so easily beset *us*, and **let us run with patience the race that is set before us, Looking unto Jesus the author and finisher of *our* faith;** who for the joy that was set before him endured the cross, despising the shame, and is set down at the right hand of the throne of God.

Philippians 3:14
I **press toward the mark for the prize** of the high calling of God in Christ Jesus.

I thought about the power of the Holy Spirit in our lives… that He came to give us POWER to do His work.

1 Corinthians 4:20
For the kingdom of God *is* not in word, but **in power**.

1 Thessalonians 1:5
For our gospel came not unto you in word only, but also **in power**, and in the Holy Ghost, and in much assurance; as ye know what manner of men we were among you for your sake.

Let the power flow.

A PLANTING OF THE LORD

Several years ago, as I was going through some very deep struggles, the Word of the Lord came so alive to me in my circumstances in a very personal way. There are no words that can describe the healing and refreshing that I experienced as the Holy Spirit applied the Word to my life. I want to share this special Word with you, because I know others have been there and need refreshing and healing. I hope it blesses your life.

> **Hosea 2: 13-24**
> 13 And I will visit upon her the days of Baalim, wherein she burned incense to them, and she decked herself with her earrings and her jewels, and she went after her lovers, and forgat me, saith the Lord.

God will help me forgive myself for my past sins where I let the lust of the flesh, the lust of the eyes, and the pride of life take over my life. He will forgive me for finding other lovers and replacing Him. He will forgive me for seeking comfort in others instead of Him. He will restore our relationship.

> 14 Therefore, behold, I will allure her, and bring her into the wilderness, and speak comfortably unto her.

On To The Prize

He will lead me to the wilderness to be there alone with Him. He will take me away from the distractions and take the distractions away from me, so I can focus on Him. He will speak tenderly and lovingly to me. He will restore my heart.

> 15 And I will give her her vineyards from thence, and the valley of Achor for a door of hope: and she shall sing there, as in the days of her youth, and as in the day when she came up out of the land of Egypt.

It is there, in the wilderness, that I will get the harvest of my soul... transformation. It is there, in the wilderness, that I will get deliverance from the past and have hope renewed. He will restore my joy.

> 16 And it shall be at that day, saith the Lord, that thou shalt call me Ishi; and shalt call me no more Baali.

He will be my "Ishi," my Husband. He will fulfill my heart. He will fulfill my needs. I will look at Him, not as a taskmaster, but as a loving Husband. He doesn't want me to "perform" good deeds to get His love. He wants to just love me and bless me. He will restore my love.

> 17 For I will take away the names of Baalim out of her mouth, and they shall no more be remembered by their name.

The love for other things that was holding me for so many years is removed from my heart. My memory of the love I had for those things will be removed. My lips will not speak the curses over my life any longer. He will restore my mind.

> 18 And in that day will I make a covenant for them with the beasts of the field, and with the fowls of heaven, and with the creeping things of the ground: and I will break the bow and the sword and the battle out of the earth, and will make them to lie down safely.

He has a covenant with His creatures and creation for me. He is always working on my behalf. He is working things out for His glory and my good. He is my Husband. He will keep me safe in the midst of the battles. He will restore my protection.

> 19 And I will betroth thee unto me for ever; yea, I will betroth thee unto me in righteousness, and in judgment, and in lovingkindness, and in mercies.

"HE" is betrothed to "me". That means that He has committed Himself to me with everything He "IS" and everything He "HAS". That is His part of this marriage. With or without my commitment, HE IS His covenant. He will restore my covenant.

> 20 I will even betroth thee unto me in faithfulness: and thou shalt know the Lord.

Because of His love and faithfulness to me, I will acknowledge Him at every opportunity. I will draw closer and closer to Him. I will share His love and compassion with those around me... those He brings into my path for His purposes. I will have many divine appointments. He will restore my witness.

> 21 And it shall come to pass in that day, I will hear, saith the Lord, I will hear the heavens, and they shall hear the earth.

He WILL respond to me. He will hear "Thy will be done on earth as it is in Heaven". He will hear what comes to His Throne and Heaven will respond. He will restore my hearing.

> 22 And the earth shall hear the corn, and the wine, and the oil; and they shall hear Jezreel.

Jezreel means "the sowing of the Lord," what "HE" has sown. I will reap the benefits. The earth and all that is in it will hear and respond to His sowing. They will see and receive His provision (corn). They will hear and see the moving of His Holy Spirit (the Wine). They will see and feel the anointing of the Holy Spirit (the Oil) through me... "the sowing of the Lord". He will restore my provision. He will restore my anointing.

> 23 And I will sow her unto me in the earth; and I will have mercy upon her that had not obtained mercy; and I will say to them which were not my people, Thou art my people; and they shall say, Thou art my God.

I am his planting. He planted me for Himself in the land. I am "the sowing of the Lord". I am what He wants to bloom and grow and flourish. He planted me because He knew I would produce a good crop. I am His and He is mine. He will restore mercy.

The day the Holy Spirit spoke this to me was one of my most blessed. Only the Holy Spirit could have done the quick work of lifting me up above all circumstances into such a place of peace and rest.

I know there are many of you who have been in situations that you thought were impossible and seemed so hopeless. I know there are many of you that have been so discouraged about choices you've made and places you been. I know there are many of you who thought God couldn't possibly restore to you what you had before. But I'm here to tell you, He will restore.

> **Joel 2:25-26**
> And I will restore to you the years that the locust hath eaten, the cankerworm, and the caterpiller, and the palmerworm, my great army which I sent among you. And ye shall eat in plenty, and be satisfied, and praise the name of the LORD your God, that hath dealt wondrously with you: and my people shall never be ashamed.

He will restore mercy.
He will restore your anointing.
He will restore your spiritual hearing.
He will restore your witness.
He will restore your covenant.
He will restore your protection.
He will restore your mind.
He will restore your love.
He will restore your joy.
He will restore your heart.
He will restore your relationship.

You will be satisfied. You will praise the Lord. He will deal wondrously with you. You will see the goodness of the Lord in the land of the living, in the land of your living.

> **Psalm 27:13**
> *I had fainted*, unless I had believed to see the goodness of the LORD in the land of the living.

Luke 1:37 - There is nothing impossible with God.

APPLYING GOD'S WORD

I was looking through some old papers from my college days and ran across something I'd written over thirty years ago. I remember how my heart was moved with promise by the Holy Spirit one day when I was at school at Trinity Bible Institute in Ellendale, North Dakota.

Genesis chapter one just bounced off the page January 5th, 1977. God knew just what I needed that day. I began to write His Word as it applied to me, for what I was going through and what He wanted to teach me. God wanted to show me how much He had me in the palm of His hand and show me how much He loved me. He wanted to show me that He had a plan for my life and show me that I was valuable to Him. I needed to know that in a strong way. I needed to see His Hand.

Put yourself into this reading and let it minister to you. I hope it blesses you, and you can apply this Word to your life.

And my life was without form and void.
And darkness and despair was upon me.
And the Spirit of God moved upon the emptiness and pain in my heart and life.

And God said, "Let there be Light and hope once again in her life". And, with no effort of my own, there was Light.

And God saw the hope that it was good.

And God divided the hope from the despair.
And God said, "Let there be a solid foundation in the center of her life of struggle and testing".

And God said, "Let her life be gathered unto one place…Jesus Christ, and let the life of victory be hers".

And God said, "Let this victorious Christian grow and bring forth fruit, yielding fruit after its own kind".

And the life grew and brought forth fruit, yielding fruit, whose seed is in itself.

And God saw that it was good.
And God said, "Let there be hope in the dark times of her life and let those times be for signs to give hope to the heart of my child".

And God said, "Let the trials and testings bring forth abundant lessons to learn for maturity and fruit".

And God allowed many great trials and small trials in my life, and each trial seemed to bring forth another after its own kind.

And God saw that it was good for me.
And God blessed them in my life… for my good and His glory.

Now that I've reread this several times, I see God's wisdom and faithfulness to me over the years. Amazing, I didn't like trials then and still don't. But, now, thirty plus years later, I have a better understanding of how the process of changing me into the image of His Son came through these trials.

This is a test. This is only a test.

FLAVOR

The wild salmon that live in the North Pacific Ocean have to fight those waters for years to get back to their spawning grounds. According to the "foodies", it is the wild salmon that have the best "flavor". They attribute that flavor to all the fighting they have to do to survive and the struggles to get back to where they were born.

Flavor is a quality of something in food which affects the taste. When someone remarks on the flavor of something, they are trying to describe the specific way it tastes.

"Flavor can also be used to describe the act of adding a taste alteration to change the taste to something. This is usually done by adding." (Wikipedia)

You wonder why you go through so much struggling in your life? God wants you to have the best flavor to this world! He is conforming us into the image of His Son, and it takes a lot of work for most of us. He is adding to the flavor of your life.

> **Romans 8:29**
> For whom He did foreknow, He also did predestinate to be conformed to the image of His Son.

He has to add His flavoring all the way through our journey to make our lives tasteful and flavor "full".

Acts 17:26-28 talks about what causes us to be more flavor "full":

> **26** And He made from one man every nation of mankind to live on all the face of the earth, having determined their appointed times and the boundaries of their habitation, **27** That they would seek God, if perhaps they might grope for Him and find Him, though He is not far from each one of us; **28** For in Him we live and move and exist, as even some of your own poets have said, "For we also are His children".

Just like the salmon, God puts us in the place we need to live. He sets the boundaries of our habitation, because He knows in which circumstances we will grow. He allows circumstances in our lives to cause us to "grope" for Him; groping as a man in total darkness, searching for a way to the light. Groping implies working for something; trying hard to reach a goal. He knows where we need to be to draw closer to Him. He knows what will cause us to grow stronger in Him. He knows what will bring out our full flavor to this world! He knows what will cause us to reflect the image of His Son to this lost and dying world.

We have that inborn nature, just like the salmon. The salmon have to get back to where they came from to fulfill their purpose in life. No matter how far away they have gone, that instinct causes them to swim against the hardest waves and tides to get back to where they belong. During the "process", something wonderful happens to them. During the fight to get back, they become very strong and full of flavor for someone else.

We have that same innate motivation inside of us as well. We have a void to fill. We have someplace we have to be. Nothing else will fulfill that void but getting back to where we belong. No matter what we try as alternatives, nothing will fill His spot. We, as His creation, strive all of our lives to get back to that place, the place of communion with God, the place of our beginning.

Every one of us is swimming upstream to find our way back to God, whether we realize it or not. God placed that need for Him in our hearts. People take many different routes, because all are innately trying to "full fill". Only He can fill His place. Just like the salmon, only when they arrive at their destination, is their life complete.

> **Ecclesiastes 3:11**
> He also has planted Eternity in men's heart and mind.

Our destination is communion with God. Only then are our lives at the best "flavor" for His Kingdom. Only when we are in communion with Him, our destination, are we the best flavor to minister to others.

We need to be flavor "full".

PROGRESSION TO DESTRUCTION

I was meditating on the story of the Prodigal Son one day and believe I had some revelation to share about our progression to destruction. It is important to learn where things go wrong, where there is a misstep, where we make wrong choices, so we can be on guard in our own lives, and be watchful for our fellowman as well. Each step is progressive, a process. But you cannot take one step without the other. They are very intertwined.

The seven steps I could see are:

1) Ungratefulness/Unthankful
2) Broken Relationship
3) Broken Fellowship
4) Resentment
5) Bitterness
6) Unteachable
7) Isolation

Just like the Prodigal Son, when we decide we know what's best for our lives, the destruction begins. We make our own plans and succumb to our own desires for what we want and think is best for us.

The first thing the Prodigal Son shows us is ungratefulness. He didn't appreciate what he had and where he was. He thought he could do better and enjoy life more his way. Then he broke relationship with those who loved and cared for him the most. He walked away from fellowship; protection and care for his soul and body. He resented his heritage and became bitter. He wanted his inheritance and wanted to see what others had to offer. No one could help him. He had to learn the hard way. No one could talk him out of it. He wouldn't listen to reason. He was unteachable for now.

He kept playing his games with friends who didn't care about him. He had fellowship, of sorts, with the wrong crowd. I say fellowship "of sorts" because the term fellowship means deeper care for one another and deeper relationship.

After all his money was gone, he was all alone. He was isolated from this new world he discovered and isolated from his old life. Alone. Ungrateful. He had broken relationships. Had broken fellowship. Resentment and bitterness had set in.

What it took for him to become teachable was isolation without anyone to care. He was doing a horrible thing for his living, slopping pigs and eating what they ate. He was a prominent Jewish descendant and never would have been called to do such a thing. He got himself into this situation because of his own decisions.

The Prodigal Son had his eyes on all the wrong things. He didn't love his father the way he should. He didn't honor his father like he should. He didn't honor His great heritage. He only wanted what the father had to give him materialistically. Had he desired the right things, like a good name, heritage, and honor, things would have been much different in his life.

> **1 John 2:15-17**
> Love not the world, neither the things that are in the world. If any man love the world, the love of the Father is not in him.
> For all that is in the world, the lust of the flesh, and the lust of the eyes, and the pride of life, is not of the Father, but is of the world. And the world passeth away, and the lust thereof: but he that doeth the will of God abideth for ever.

Are we fulfilling the lust of our flesh, the lust of our eyes, or our pride of life? Be on guard. That is the slippery slope to destruction.

The Bible tells us to "keep and guard your heart with all diligence and above all that you guard your heart, for out of it flow the springs of life" (Proverbs 4:23). If you don't guard your heart, the world will creep in and your focus will be off. When our focus gets off fellowship with the Father and His saints, the destruction begins. It's very subtle. The fellowship with the Father doesn't just break overnight. The fellowship with our brothers and sisters doesn't just break suddenly… unless we get offended and walk away.

We withdraw from the normal fellowship for many reasons. We get offended and cut off relationships. We get too busy… even doing good. If the enemy gets us too busy for fellowship and relationships, he knows it will weaken us. He knows that as we encourage each other so we will be stronger.

> **1 Thessalonians 5:11**
> Therefore comfort yourselves together, and edify one another, even as also ye do.

> **Romans 14:19**
> Let us therefore follow after the things which make for peace, and things wherewith one may edify another.

We get sidetracked… distraction… one of the enemy's favorite tactics. Our earthly circumstances distract us from our focus on God's power and Truth. We surround ourselves with things and/or people that are easy to be around so no "iron sharpens iron; so a man sharpens the countenance of his friend" (Proverbs 27:17). We decide not to love the unlovely and make our lives as comfortable as possible. After all, we're tired of the battling, right?

If the fellowship doesn't grow, the relationships weaken. When the fellowship is broken, the relationships remain broken as well. We withdraw from our fellowship with God and those He has placed in our lives to strengthen us. It then doesn't take much to have broken relationships, because other works of the flesh have the open door to creep into our lives full force.

We then get resentful and bitter. Someone didn't treat us right. Someone hurt us. We resent their authority. We resent their behavior. We judge them. That root of bitterness begins to grow the minute any resentment is present. We complain about their behavior or our circumstances, etc. That is ingratitude. We become ungrateful for the things God has done through other people and even become ungrateful to Him for all He has done for us. We withdraw even more and go further away from our "source" of strength… our Father and the people He brought into our lives.

When a person has reached this point, they are unteachable. There is nothing humanly possible you can do. You pray and love them unconditionally, but the Holy Spirit has to break them. So, you might as well shut your mouth. Whatever you say will bring up more judgment and resentment in them. They will not "receive" your words into their spirit. When you do open your mouth, be sure you are being used as an instrument of the Holy Spirit.

They will isolate themselves, maybe not physically, but they are behind their walls nonetheless… insulating and isolating. They have become the Prodigal Son. But this isolation, as you will see, isn't always a bad thing.

I'm reminded of a phrase in **1 Kings 12: 24**

> Thus said the Lord, Ye shall not go up, nor fight against your brethren the children of Israel: return every man to his house; **for this thing is from me.** They hearkened therefore to the word of the Lord, and returned to depart, according to the Word of the Lord.

"For this thing is from me". The division in the camp? The division in the House of Israel? Yes! It's for His purposes. He is the only One Who knows what it will take for some people to turn around. He is the only One Who knows what it will take to form them into the image of His Son.

In this isolation, the Prodigal Son, "came to himself" or "came to the end of himself". That's where we all need to be. Only when we come to the end of "self", do we go back to the Father and stop trying to do it ourselves. No amount of counseling or deliverance can ever crucify the flesh. That is a decision we have to make on our own on a regular basis. We must "daily" crucify the flesh so we won't get off course by the pride of life, the lust of the eyes, and the lust of the flesh… down the road to destruction.

> **Luke 9:23**
> And he said to them all, If any man will come after me, let him deny himself, and take up his cross daily, and follow me.

Don't head down that road to destruction. It is a progression. To keep intact in our relationship with God and fellowship with people, we need to remain grateful.

> **Psalm 26:6-8**
> [6] I will wash mine hands in innocency: so will I compass thine altar, O LORD: [7] That I may publish with the voice of thanksgiving, and tell of all thy wondrous works. [8] LORD, I have loved the habitation of thy house, and the place where thine honour dwelleth.

After the Prodigal Son's adventures, I believe he would be shouting these verses from his heart to the top of his voice to all who would listen. He finally came to the place where now he was full of thanksgiving for what he had, where he was, and who he was. He came to the place where now he honored his father and the dwelling place he had for him. He came to the place where he could have ears to hear and eyes to see all his inheritance and heritage.

God longs for us all to get to that place in our lives where we let Psalms 26 be the cry of our existence. God longs for us to be grateful and offer thanksgiving continually. God longs for us all to spend time with Him. God longs for us all to speak out of all His wondrous works. God longs for us all to honor Him. God longs for us to come to the place where we appreciate and understand who we are in Him and all we have in Him. We have an heritage like none other. We are children of The Almighty God.

Remain grateful.

Remain in relationship.

Remain in fellowship.

Remain forgiving.

Remain teachable.

Avoid the path of the Prodigal Son.

GRAVITATIONAL PULL

Looking out the airplane window, everything seems so small. I say "seems" because none of the things I'm looking at have changed a bit. I'm just higher and seeing them from a different perspective. I'm farther removed from them and get a completely different picture of what they look like and how they all look together.

When I'm looking from the airplane window, all that I'm looking at reminds me of things I've seen before in my other travels. The farther up the plane goes, the location becomes more unrecognizable. Even though I've traveled there on the ground and at different times by plane or train, soon it becomes unrecognizable. From up here, things just don't look the same. It's hard to identify. Even though it's familiar, I can't specifically identify anything after awhile.

The colors aren't as bright up here either, because there is a haze that develops. Even if there aren't clouds to block the view, I rise into an atmosphere that has changed. As I'm rising, the temperature and the wind velocity change. All the elements of a different atmosphere change how I see things. The things that looked so vibrant and attractive when I was down among them, aren't as colorful and attractive from up here because of the change in atmosphere.

How does that all apply to my life? I have to see things from the atmosphere of God's presence, away from this world, in heavenly places with Him. I need to be in His atmosphere, His presence to see from the right perspective. Rising above to heavenly places with Christ, keeps us focused on the right things.

> **Ephesians 2:5-7**
> [5] Even when we were dead in sins, [he] hath quickened us together with Christ, (by grace ye are saved;) [6] And hath raised us up together, and made us sit together in heavenly places in Christ Jesus: [7] That in the ages to come he might shew the exceeding riches of his grace in his kindness toward us through Christ Jesus.

The closer we get to God, the attractiveness of this world dims. Things of this world will become hazy, and we won't be drawn to them. As we get farther from the things of this earth, the gravitational pull begins to weaken. The closer we get to God, the draw of the world doesn't have as much grip on us.

> **1 John 2:15-16**
> Love not the world, neither the things that are in the world. If any man love the world, the love of the Father is not in him. For all that is in the world, the lust of the flesh, and the lust of the eyes, and the pride of life, is not of the Father, but is of the world.

Isn't that what we want? The world's pull to lose its grip on us. To be heavenly minded is what keeps us focused on the right things. Our lust of the eyes and our flesh, our pride, that's what causes all the problems. We are drawn away by our own lusts. That gravitational pull of this world tries to draw us away from rising up to heavenly places.

Keeping our eyes and heart on things above will weaken that pull. Keeping our eyes and heart on things above will strengthen our heavenly pull. That breaks it down pretty simply.

How do you do that?

Philippians 4:8
Finally, brethren, whatsoever things are true, whatsoever things are honest, whatsoever things are just, whatsoever things are pure, whatsoever things are lovely, whatsoever things are of good report; if there be any virtue, and if there be any praise, think on these things.

Romans 12:1-2
I beseech you therefore, brethren, by the mercies of God, that ye present your bodies a living sacrifice, holy, acceptable unto God, which is your reasonable service. 2 And be not conformed to this world: but be ye transformed by the renewing of your mind, that ye may prove what is that good, and acceptable, and perfect, will of God.

Change your thinking: an intentional action.

Ephesians 4:21-23
21 If so be that ye have heard him, and have been taught by him, as the truth is in Jesus: 22 That ye put off concerning the former conversation the old man, which is corrupt according to the deceitful lusts; 23 And be renewed in the spirit of your mind;

Colossians 3:8-10
8 But now ye also put off all these; anger, wrath, malice, blasphemy, filthy communication out of your mouth. 9 Lie not one to another, seeing that ye have put off the old man with his deeds; 10 And have put on the new man, which is renewed in knowledge after the image of him that created him:

Put off the old behavior. You have to decide to change your behavior. You have to make better choices. An intentional action.

Live intentionally.

HEARING GOD

There are several things that God's Word instructs us to do to make sure we are hearing "HIS" voice and not the voice of the enemy of our souls, the world, or our own voice. Is there a litmus test? Yes. Do we really hear God? He tells us that "My sheep hear my voice", in John 10:27. He gave us safeguards to make sure we heard correctly. He knows we are but flesh.

The Bible tells us that "The heart is deceitful and desperately wicked, who can know it?" (**Jeremiah 17:9**). I don't trust myself to hear God's voice perfectly on all things. God already told me I would hear many voices and that my heart gets in the way.

> **1 John 4:1**
> Beloved, believe not every spirit, but try the spirits whether they are of God.

My mind and emotions and experiences many times get in the way of hearing clearly to make proper decisions. We need to follow the safeguards laid out in God's Word.

Did He give me an answer to what I was praying for?

> **Luke 11:11-13**
> If a son shall ask bread of any of you that is a father, will he give him a stone? Or if he ask a fish, will he for a fish give him a serpent? Or if he shall ask an egg, will he offer him a scorpion? If ye then, being evil, know how to give good gifts unto your children: how much more shall your

heavenly Father give the Holy Spirit to them that ask him?

John 16:13
He will guide you into all truth.

He won't give you a counterfeit answer. He will say yes, no or wait. The devil is the one who tries to quickly slip in a counterfeit or substitute. Be on guard and wait for clarity and confirmation. Everything that looks like a "good gift" from above, may be a substitute. Run down the checklist in His Word.

Did I pray in faith?

Hebrews 11:6
But without faith it is impossible to please Him: for He that cometh to God must believe that He is, and the He is a rewarder of them that diligently seek Him.

Matthew 21:22
And all things, whatsoever you shall ask in prayer, believing, you shall receive.

Did I pray in agreement with someone?

Matthew 18:19
Where two agree as touching any one thing it shall be done.

The Bible says that "one puts a thousand to flight, but two puts ten thousand to flight", **(Deuteronomy 32:30).** Praying in agreement is ten times stronger!

Did I let someone "bear my burden and so fulfill the law of Christ" (Galatians 6:2)?

We need to share our burdens and prayers requests with one another. God wants us to come together, care for one another, and stand in the gap for one another. God will honor that sacrifice.

Did I seek wise, Godly counsel?

Proverbs 15:22
Without counsel purposes are disappointed: but in the multitude of counselors they are established.

Proverbs 1:5
A wise man will hear, and will increase learning; and a man of understanding shall attain unto wise counsels.

Proverbs 12:15
The way of a fool is right in his own eyes: but he that hearkeneth unto counsel is wise.

Proverbs 20:18
Every purpose is established by counsel: and with good advice make war.

Proverbs 11:14
Where no counsel is, the people fall: but in the multitude of counselors there is safety.

Did I seek confirmation?

Corinthians 13:1
In the mouth of two or three witnesses shall every word be established.

Is there peace?

Follow peace.

Timothy 2:22
Flee also youthful lusts: but follow righteousness, faith, charity, peace, with them that call on the Lord out of a pure heart.

Hebrews 12:14
Follow peace with all men, and holiness, without which no man shall see the Lord.

In the times we are living, with all the voices, even though we hear His voice, the Bible tells us that even the very elect will be deceived.

Matthew 24:24
For there shall arise false Christs, and false prophets, and shall show great signs and wonders; insomuch that, if it were possible, they shall deceive the very elect.

The Word has given us safety nets so we can know His voice in decisions we make. So, for example, if someone tells me they spend the weekend alone with God, and God gave them direction about something, I want to hear what God has said to them. But I also want to know if they followed His safeguards in their decisions as well. Because, they were also alone with their own thoughts with plenty of time to think and dwell on situations, people, circumstances, etc. His Word is His Word…verbal, written, or by spiritual impressions. His Word is alive inside of us. Let's confirm His Word to make sure we are walking in His Word.

If someone has to give reasons and excuses along with "hearing from God" or "hearing His voice", are they looking at circumstances? Circumstances are not the litmus test of God's voice. Did they really hear Him? Or are they following experiences, feelings or heart?…that deceitful thing…that desperately wicked thing.

Just remember, whatever the situation is in your life, you can't take a misstep in direction that He can't fix. He will get us back on the narrow path if we submit to Him and let "His Word be a lamp unto our feet and a light unto our path" (**Psalm 119:105**).

Let His "Word" lead you.

HARD LESSON

One of the hardest lessons I've had to learn is that you can't help someone who really doesn't want help. You can't give enough love to someone who won't receive love. You can't feed someone who just won't eat. The old saying, "You can lead a horse to water, but you can't make him drink", has been shown to me in full force. If someone doesn't hunger and thirst after righteousness, you can't make it happen. It's all about their choices.

They "say" they want help, but their actions aren't showing they are really hungry and thirsty for righteousness. They want their lives to change, but they don't want to change. They want their circumstances to change, but they don't want to change. They want the pain to stop, but they don't want to change. They don't want to be responsible for any of the problem, because they don't want to change. They aren't devouring the Word and hearing those that God has sent into their lives to help them.

They won't receive encouragement. They won't receive love. They definitely won't accept correction and instruction in righteousness. They want help…but not to change. They want help to get comfortable with their pain instead of being healed from their pain. They don't want to take the necessary steps to change.

My Bible tells me the only way to change or be transformed is by the renewing of the mind (**Romans 12:2**), by the washing of the water of the Word (**Ephesians 5:26**). When you see transformation in someone's life, you know that they are washing with the Word.

Their mind is being renewed. Therefore, their lives are being transformed.

> **Matthew 25:34-40** tells us we are to clothe, feed, and house those who need help. He will bless us for helping. But, He also tells us, if they claim to be His child, there are expectations of behavior. They must show fruit and grow in the grace and knowledge of the Lord Jesus Christ. There does come a time to release someone. There does come a time that you are not responsible anymore. The Bible tells us what to do.

> **Galatians 6:1**
> Brethren, if a man be overtaken in a fault, ye which are spiritual, restore such an one in the spirit of meekness; considering thyself, lest thou also be tempted.

We are our brother's keeper. The Bible gives us instructions that we are to speak to them if they are going the wrong way. If we don't, their blood is on our hands. Once you have spoken to them about it and they continues to sin, you are no longer responsible.

The Holy Spirit shows us in the Word how Jesus handled these situations. The Prodigal Son wasn't chased down by the Father. The Father had to wait for him to return after "he came to himself". Had someone been there all the time to rescue that boy out of the pigpen and kept bailing him out, he would have remained too comfortable to make a change. Sometimes we get in God's way and do the same, make them too comfortable to make a change.

> **Acts 17:26-27**
> And He made from one man every nation of mankind to live on all the face of the earth, having determined their appointed times and the boundaries of their habitation, That they would seek God, if perhaps they might grope for Him and find Him, though He is not far from each one of us;

God knows the "place" or what the bounds of our habitation need to be that will cause us to seek after Him. We need to be in a place that causes us to grope for Him, many times, in desperation, so we can know Who our Source is and know that He is working all things out for our good and His glory.

Jesus shared His love and truth. If they didn't "hear" Him, He shook the dust from His feet and went onto the next place. People who came "to" Him because they wanted healing and deliverance, were healed and delivered. If someone says they want it but don't come to Him, don't grope for Him, aren't hungry enough for Him, aren't desperate enough for Him… it won't happen. They won't be filled. They won't be healed. They won't be delivered. You've probably heard the saying, "Seek the Healer, not the healing" or "Seek the Deliverer, not the deliverance"…therein lies your healing… drawing closer to Him… being transformed in His Presence.

It's very heartbreaking when you can see the potential in someone, yet they desire to stay in that place of comfort and complacency. It's very heartbreaking when you see the pain that Jesus wants to heal, and they won't let you in to help them. It's so difficult to watch someone self-destruct by the words of their mouth, knowing that they will have to reap what they are sowing. It's not easy knowing they are rebelling against God's authority and those He put in authority, because they have to reap what they've sown. Galatians 6:7 states: "Be not deceived, God is not mocked. Whatsoever a man sows that shall he also reap".

There comes a time that you have to let them go. They have to learn hard lessons. We get in the way of God's work so many times. There are so many times Christians believe they are to "rescue" someone out of a situation, thinking they are doing the right thing. However, much of time the "mercy" gift isn't really in operation. It is compassion, but not Spirit-led action.

Sometimes mercy and compassion don't look like mercy and compassion. Real mercy is shown by letting God bring them to a place that will cause them to seek after Him and become desperate for Him. If we step in and give them comfort and try to solve all their problems, their comfort will negate the desperateness for Him. Sometimes you have to let them walk right into very painful situations.

Pray before you act. Wait to hear direction before you act. Get wise, Godly counsel before you act.

Get out of God's way.

LEADERSHIP

1 Samuel 18:1,2,5
When David had finished speaking to Saul, the soul of Jonathan was knit with the soul of David, and Jonathan loved him as his own life. Saul took David that day and would not let him return to his father's house. And David went out wherever Saul sent him, and he prospered and behaved himself wisely; and Saul set him over the men of war. And it was satisfactory both to the people and to Saul's servants.

David had just killed Goliath and presented himself to King Saul. Verse 2 tells us that his acts of faith and obedience "brought him before great men" and that "his gift made room for him" **(Proverbs 18:16).** He was entering a level of training to become the man he needed to be to fulfill his destiny… King.

David was under Saul's leadership, no matter how flawed it was. God placed David there for a time of training and internship. In Matthew, Jesus told the people to listen and learn from the Scribes and Pharisees. What they were teaching was right and they should do what the Scribes and Pharisees SAY, but don't DO what they DO. Wouldn't it be nice to be under the leadership of a good king, a man of great character, a man with a heart after God? Well it doesn't always happen that way. Because of this, we should look at this example in God's Word carefully.

David learned a great deal of what he needed for future kingship, even under poor leadership, under a rebellious, self-centered King Saul. David followed the Lord's leading on a daily basis in obedience to the king, even though he knew he was anointed to be king. He "behaved himself wisely" and waited on the Lord by "actively serving" until his place in history would be settled. He honored the Kingship, even though he knew that King Saul wasn't a man of honor. God place Saul in that role, and we are blessed when we give honor to whom honor is due **(Romans 13:7)**. David knew that principle and practiced it at every level of his journey and at every opportunity.

So, no matter what is happening in the "head", we still can learn so many important lessons and get valuable training for the days ahead. Bless God for where you are. Be full of thanksgiving and praise Him for your situation. Only God knows what the blessing and outflow from your life will be for enduring these situations.

Saul treated David badly… yet he trusted him to do things he didn't trust anybody else to do. He knew David's character was good and stable.

> **1 Samuel 18:12-16**
> Saul was afraid of David because the Lord was with him but had departed from Saul. So Saul removed him from his presence and made him a commander of a thousand. And he went out and came in before the people. And David had success in all his undertakings, for the Lord was with him. And when Saul saw that he had great success, he stood in fearful awe of him. But all Israel and Judah loved David, for he went out and came in before them.

Saul's fear of David's anointing didn't stop Saul from trying to destroy this good man. You may run into the same situation in your own life or may have already seen it in the lives of your friends.

The works of the flesh were very evident in Saul's life. He was very jealous of David. The Bible tells us that when envy and jealousy are present, so are all the other works of the flesh **(James 3:16)**. It's not a pretty picture. It must have seemed like his problems were never going to end, but David remained steadfast in following God's ways. He went through physical and personal attacks. He had to go into hiding. It wasn't easy for David. It was a very hard seven years before he became king and then he wasn't fully king at that point. More had to transpire to get him into full position. But, God had someone in his corner… Jonathan.

Through this difficult time in David's life, he had an armor-bearer and friend. God sends those along side of us in life to help us. We in turn help them. We are to be by each others' side to help each other along, especially in difficult times. We are to "bear one another's burdens" **(Galatians 6:2)** and to "encourage each other daily in the Lord" **(Hebrews 3:13).** That's the only way we will make it to the fulfillment of God's purpose for us on this planet. Are you holding up the progress of someone else. Or are they in battles alone unnecessarily because you are failing to lift them up?

Just like David, there may not be very many at our side at times, but numbers don't matter. Here is where the "quality" vs. "quantity" factor really applies. It's the quality of the relationships, not the quantity, that help us stand and not fall. Every one needs an "Aaron and Hur" to hold us up in battle.

Just as in David's situation, the time comes when the ministry relationship has to end. The grace for the time under that leadership lifts, and we must take our destiny position and/or sometimes move on to instruction under another leader. Listen to God carefully. He will bring you out into that purpose as you walk with integrity and "behave yourself wisely".

Behave yourself wisely.

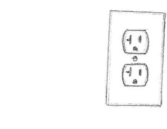

DISCONNECTED

On TV a few years ago, I heard someone say, "You need feedback from others to get in touch with your reality." Another way of saying that is, if you stay disconnected from others, you will not be in touch with reality. I know that's hard for some people to hear because they think they don't need anyone and they're doing just fine. It is a very dangerous place to be on so many levels.

Think about a power cord. The intent of the cord is to connect to the electricity to give the object power to run as the manufacturer intended. By staying connected to the Holy Spirit, we hopefully won't fall short of displaying God's glory in our day to day operations. By staying connected with each other, we will have more power to accomplish what God has intended for us.

The Bible tells us that where two or more agree on any one thing it shall be done. That means we are connected. The Bible tells us that one puts a thousand to flight and two puts ten thousand to flight. That tells me if we stay connected, we are ten times stronger. The Bible calls us a Body. The Body parts connected as a whole can get things done that being disconnected would never accomplish. A finger couldn't operate without the hand helping it. The hand cannot operate without the arm moving it in the right direction. We need to be connected to each other. We are THE BODY for His Kingdom purposes.

It is in our connectedness with people where we are filled and healed (James 5:16). We need to PRACTICE connection. It's not always the natural thing to do, so we have to work at it. We have to do it "on purpose". Because we're gun-shy from all the disappointments in life and all the hurts we've encountered along the way, disconnection seems the best thing to do to prevent further disappointment. It's the wrong way to go. From personal experience, I can tell you it's the worst thing to do in this Christian walk. I attended a church for over a year and met no one. I sat in the services week after week and didn't reach out to meet anyone or even try to establish any relationships. It's not healthy.

Disconnection hurts you in so many ways. You can't be the person you were meant to be from the foundations of this world. Without allowing others to invest in your life, you won't learn and grow as it was intended when you were formed in your mother's womb.

So, if you know someone who doesn't "connect" with many people, they are very out of touch with reality. They have been wounded and don't want to hear what anyone has to say. They don't want to hurt anymore, so they disconnect. Disconnection is losing your lifeline. Disconnection is losing your power source. God put us on this earth for each other. We are created to be relational.

Get connected to others and stay connected.

MOUNTAINS

From my view up here in the airplane, some mountains don't look so big. They actually look like something that could be "plucked up and thrown into the sea".

> **Mark 11:23**
> For verily I say unto you, That whosoever shall say unto this mountain, Be thou removed, and be thou cast into the sea; and shall not doubt in his heart, but shall believe that those things which he saith shall come to pass; he shall have whatsoever he saith.

So it's got to be our perspective then. When we are at the foot of a mountain looking up, its size is overwhelming. When we are on the mountain, it's overwhelming, but we only see a small part of it, so it's not as bad. When we are above the mountain, it looks much smaller.

So how do we get a different perspective?

We have to see differently. We have to understand God's perspective.

> **Philippians 2:5**
> Let this mind be in you, which was also in Christ Jesus:

Our minds have to be transformed.

Romans 12:2
And be not conformed to this world: but be ye transformed by the renewing of your mind, that ye may prove what is that good, and acceptable, and perfect, will of God.

Then we will see as He sees. We won't see things as we used to see them anymore. Things that looked so big won't look so big anymore. Things that used to overwhelm us won't overwhelm us any longer.

We are to have the same mind in us that was in Christ Jesus. Then we will see from His perspective.

1 Corinthians 2:16
For who hath known the mind of the Lord, that he may instruct him? But we have the mind of Christ.

Let this mind be in you that is in Christ Jesus.

A SUBTLE SIN

According to the following Scripture, many of us have repenting to do. Many of us have ourselves on our mind too much. Some of us have the "us four and no more" mentality. God is searching for those who will step outside their comfort zone, outside the familiar, and reach far beyond themselves to stretch.

> **1 Samuel 12:23**
> Moreover, as for me, far be it from me that I should sin against the Lord by ceasing to pray for you; but I will instruct you in the good and right way.

Sinning by ceasing to pray for someone?... hmmmmmm.

We are tired. We have other things on our minds. Our hearts are full of something other than compassion for others. To get beyond that, we have to deny ourselves daily and frequently during the day. We need to choose not to do how we "feel", but what is right in the sight of God according to His Word.

> **Luke 9:23**
> And he said to them all, If any man will come after me, let him deny himself, and take up his cross daily, and follow me.

> **Galatians 5:24**
> And they that are Christ's have crucified the flesh with the affections and lusts.

There is no such thing as a coincidence. God allows people to come across our paths everyday for a reason. If you weren't able to share your faith with them or minister to them in some way, then perhaps God brought them across your path so that you would lift them up before Him. Maybe they have no one in their life to pray for them. You were chosen to cross their path.

Not every situation is alike. Not every prayer is alike. Not every need is alike. Hear the Holy Spirit and pray. You were privileged to be used by God. Take every opportunity, no matter how small and insignificant you think it is.

Think on those things.

THE LION OF JUDAH

I was watching a program about African animals and heard the Holy Spirit speak to me about something that was going on during the program. I'm sure you've seen similar programs and maybe even the same program as I watched. Have you noticed how all the animals scatter when the lion comes around? Even if the lion isn't hungry at the time, they still scatter. Maybe he's just going to the watering hole. It doesn't matter. In his presence, all other animals scatter except, of course, those in his den.

The lion is the king of the jungle. It's just something the other animals know. It was born in them to fear the king of the jungle.

Then I started thinking about The Lion of Judah. Judah means "praise". Remember the lion causes anything in its way to scatter. So, doesn't it bless you to know that our "Judah", our "praise", causes those things in our way to scatter? He makes a path for our provision.

Psalm 68:1
Let God arise, let His enemies be scattered: let them also that hate Him flee before Him.

This scenario made me think of the effect of praise on the main enemy of our souls.

Psalm 8:2
Out of the mouth of babes and sucklings hast thou ordained strength because of thine enemies, that thou mightest still the enemy and the avenger.

The NIV translation of the Bible gives us a better understanding of what those words actually mean:

Through the praise of children and infants you have established a stronghold against your enemies, to **silence the foe** and the avenger.

The Bible tells us that praise "stills" the enemy. That means it "paralyzes" him in that moment when we are praising God.

We are to offer up praise continually.

Psalm 34:1
A Psalm of David, when he changed his behaviour before Abimelech; who drove him away, and he departed. I will bless the LORD at all times: his praise *shall* continually *be* in my mouth.

Hebrews 13:15
By him therefore let us offer the sacrifice of praise to God continually, that is, the fruit of *our* lips giving thanks to his name.

God knows the effect that praise has on our lives and on the enemy.

Here is a visual that I have used to teach. It gets the point across very well. Picture this with me. Someone walking around with every piece of valuable jewelry hanging from the wrists, fingers, ears, neck, ankles: diamonds, sapphires, all the most valuable jewels on earth in large quantities. Then see the enemy and his imps attacking and stealing from that person; stealing everything that they own of value or that was valuable to them.

Then see this person again walking around with every piece of valuable jewelry. But this time, their hands are raised in praise, their lips are praising the Lord continually. The enemy and his imps are around, but paralyzed with every syllable of praise. The person takes a breath and the enemy takes a step. But, as the person keeps praising, they gain more and more ground and are far ahead of the enemy.

> **John 10:10**
> The thief cometh not, but for to steal, and to kill, and to destroy: I am come that they might have life, and that they might have *it* more abundantly.

Our enemy never gives up trying to steal and kill and destroy, but as we keep praising, we have that life abundant that Jesus said was ours.

Scatter your enemies with PRAISE.

LUKEWARM

I was thinking of that familiar Scripture in Revelation about being lukewarm.

> **Revelation 3:16**
> So then because thou art lukewarm, and neither cold nor hot, I will spue thee out of my mouth.

I have heard many sermons throughout my lifetime about this verse. Most sermons referenced the fact that we need to be on fire for God - HOT - or on the other hand, be brave enough to admit you don't want anything to do with God - COLD. If you just float along and go through the motions and try to fake your walk with God, you make God sick enough to throw up -LUKEWARM. That was the extent of that verse's interpretation as I was growing up.

As I studied and meditated on this subject, I got a clearer picture of what God may have been saying to us. Being in the medical field and knowing some science and biology, this took on a different meaning for me.

Hot and cold. Those are very common and relevant terms in the medical field. Lukewarm water isn't used for much. You need hotter salt water to swish in your mouth to help heal a mouth wound or clean up a mess. You need cool water to pour over burns or irrigate lacerations or other wounds. Lukewarm water is used to flush out the ears. Now that is saying something. We have to have ears to hear what the Spirit is saying to the Church today. It takes ears to hear what the Spirit is saying to us in our daily walk with God.

Lukewarm water causes nausea when you drink it. Lukewarm water without a source of fresh water will become stagnate and sit there growing bacteria of many different species.

Cold water is refreshing and soothing. Drinking a nice cold drink refreshes and restores energy. A cool shower or pool brings great refreshing in the hot and dry times. God wants His children to bring refreshing to others.

Hot water is cleansing and soothing. Once someone soaks in hot water, tension is gone, muscle cramps are relieved, and skin is cleansed of impurities. God wants us to be able to lead people into cleansing, healing, and restoration.

So, when I think about how God hates the LUKEWARM, I'm sure He wants us to be HOT and COLD in His Kingdom, being productive citizens.

Reminds me of the story of the talents in Matthew 25. This may well be about using what He has given us, the gifts, talents, abilities, resources, to refresh and restore others.

Be HOT and COLD.

ROAD SIGNS

I've done a lot of driving all over this country for many years. There are so many different road signs to understand and follow. I learned that I need to pay close attention to those signs. All are of great value for warning us of what is ahead or instructing us of what we need to do for our safety and the safety of others. They help us get to our intended destination… also very important.

They are building new roads and repairing old roads constantly, so we have to be on the lookout for change. We need a current roadmap to keep up with those changes. The road atlas from five years ago won't help us now. The old map is going to mislead you. Even the GPS cannot keep up with the newest changes. So we still have to watch the signs carefully.

Road signs are very important to follow even when it doesn't seem right. Many times we've been through a certain area so many times that the new sign doesn't make sense to us. It's familiar territory, and we think we could navigate it with our eyes closed. Not a good idea. We cannot get too familiar, because, again, things are always changing. Someone different is always watching and may follow. We can lead someone astray and not even be aware.

There are detour signs that must be followed, or we will cause ourselves and many others more problems. You see, no matter what you do, it never affects just you. It could even be dangerous and life-threatening if we don't obey the signs. We don't need more problems. We don't want to cause an accident, hold up traffic, or cause yet another detour for those following us.

If you are in unfamiliar territory, others' advice and direction is very important. It is even more imperative that we pay closer attention.

Our walk with God is like following road signs. If we aren't careful, we will cause another person to lose their direction, because someone is always following us on the road. If we aren't following God's direction by His Word and the voice of the Holy Spirit, we can cause someone else to go off track. We never travel alone.

We have our built in GPS, the Holy Spirit, when we belong to Christ but we still get sidetracked. The cares of this world, our circumstances in life, can get us sidetracked. That's why we need others in the Body of Christ. They are traveling this road with us and maybe can hear more clearly at a particular time than we can. And the reverse is true. God knows we are flesh, and that our spirits are willing, but life overwhelms us at times.

> **Matthew 26:41**
> Watch and pray, that ye enter not into temptation: the spirit indeed *is* willing, but the flesh *is* weak.

We must stay in God's Word, reading, studying, meditating, listening, and hearing.

Psalm 119:11
Thy word have I hid in mine heart, that I might not sin against thee.

We must pray for His direction and ask for wisdom. We must ask the Holy Spirit to apply the Word to our lives.

Things may be so familiar to us, because we've walked with the Lord many years. Those following us may have not been walking with God very long. Our familiarity may give them the wrong ideas about walking with the Lord or may lead to taking the things of God for granted. We need to always be careful to be full of gratitude in all things and listen no matter how familiar things seem. Things are always changing. Situations are never exactly the same. God is always speaking to us, and He says He wants to do a new thing. I want to be a part of that "new thing" at any time.

Be on the lookout for change.

SERVANTHOOD

Jesus said He came to be a servant. Paul the Apostle said he was servant to all that he might win some. We are to follow these examples in all things.

> **I Corinthians 9:19**
> For though I be free from all *men*, yet have I made myself servant unto all, that I might gain the more.

We are to serve one another in love. So many times, that's the missing part… "love".

> **Galatians 5:13**
> For, brethren, ye have been called unto liberty; only *use* not liberty for an occasion to the flesh, but by love serve one another.

Many times we "do" things out of obligation to others or out of guilt or to cover our tracks in some way. That's not what God has called us to do. He said to serve one another in love, preferring the other person above ourselves.

> **Ephesians 5:21**
> Submitting yourselves one to another in the fear of God.

> **Romans 12:10**
> *Be* kindly affectioned one to another with brotherly love; in honour preferring one another;

Through observation you can obtain a lot of knowledge, but better yet, a lot of understanding. When people really love each other and have "relationship", it is a joy for them to give of their time and energy. It's a pleasure for them to serve one another.

I loved to be with this older couple from our church. They were married over fifty years and were so kind and considerate to each other. They always had that twinkle in their eyes for each other. It was such a blessing to behold, especially in this day and age when so many don't have that kind of relationship God intended for us. I would spend as much time with them as I could, because they were such a good example of what Christ meant in His Word. The man told us that he "cared" for her more deeply every day. It was that his kindness and caring and concern grew deeper for her as the days went on. He said he couldn't really explain it.

That's the example for the Body of Christ. When you see others "serving" in the church building, but with an "attitude", that shows the lack of the "intimacy" of love. It shows lack of "relationship"... not only "relationship" with that person, but also "relationship" with the Lover of our souls.

This older couple had intimacy with the Father and therefore, with each other on a level many cannot comprehend. It's a sure-fire way to check your "love-tank" level. If you don't enjoy "doing" for others, or a particular "other", then you have a "love" issue. You're too self-absorbed, self-focused, and selfish for many reasons maybe, but not of importance in the big KINGDOM picture. It's not "what about me", it's about "others". Our woundedness prevents us from doing good unto all men, but we need not take that into consideration at all. Keep our eyes focuses on God, His Word, and His commands. He will increase, you will decrease... and just maybe, in the midst of it all, you will be healed of your woundedness.

How can I bless God and bless others? Through a servant's heart, a heart we are all supposed to have for this world.

We have a call to servanthood.

DIFFICULT RELATIONSHIPS

1 Samuel 24 tells the story of David confronting Saul about their relationship. He practiced the New Testament Scriptures in Matthew 5 and 18 before they were in ink. If we know someone has a problem with us, we need to go to them and try to be reconciled with them. We need to ask forgiveness. David knew his "brother had ought against him", so he went to him. And in this story in chapter 24, he finally had the safe opportunity to confront Saul. It is about "God's timing" in these situations.

> **1 Samuel 24**
> ² Then Saul took three thousand chosen men out of all Israel, and went to seek David and his men upon the rocks of the wild goats. ³ And he came to the sheepcotes by the way, where was a cave; and Saul went in to cover his feet: and David and his men remained in the sides of the cave. ⁴ And the men of David said unto him, Behold the day of which the LORD said unto thee, Behold, I will deliver thine enemy into thine hand, that thou mayest do to him as it shall seem good unto thee. Then David arose, and cut off the skirt of Saul's robe privily. ⁵ And it came to pass afterward, that David's heart smote him, because he had cut off Saul's skirt. ⁶ And he said unto his men, The LORD forbid that I should do this thing unto my master, the LORD's anointed, to stretch forth mine hand against him, seeing he is the anointed of the LORD. ⁷ So David stayed his servants with these words, and suffered them not to rise against Saul. But Saul rose up out of the cave, and went on his way. ⁸ David also arose afterward, and went out of the cave, and cried after Saul, saying, My lord the king. And when Saul looked behind

him, David stooped with his face to the earth, and bowed himself. ⁹ And David said to Saul, Wherefore hearest thou men's words, saying, Behold, David seeketh thy hurt? ¹⁰ Behold, this day thine eyes have seen how that the LORD had delivered thee to day into mine hand in the cave: and some bade me kill thee: but mine eye spared thee; and I said, I will not put forth mine hand against my lord; for he is the LORD's anointed.
¹¹ Moreover, my father, see, yea, see the skirt of thy robe in my hand: for in that I cut off the skirt of thy robe, and killed thee not, know thou and see that there is neither evil nor transgression in mine hand, and I have not sinned against thee; yet thou huntest my soul to take it.
¹² The LORD judge between me and thee, and the LORD avenge me of thee: but mine hand shall not be upon thee. ¹⁵ The LORD therefore be judge, and judge between me and thee, and see, and plead my cause, and deliver me out of thine hand. ¹⁶ And it came to pass, when David had made an end of speaking these words unto Saul, that Saul said, Is this thy voice, my son David? And Saul lifted up his voice, and wept.¹⁷ And he said to David, Thou art more righteous than I: for thou hast rewarded me good, whereas I have rewarded thee evil. ¹⁸ And thou hast shewed this day how that thou hast dealt well with me: forasmuch as when the LORD had delivered me into thine hand, thou killedst me not. ¹⁹ For if a man find his enemy, will he let him go well away? wherefore the LORD reward thee good for that thou hast done unto me this day. ²⁰ And now, behold, I know well that thou shalt surely be king, and that the kingdom of Israel shall be established in thine hand. ²¹ Swear now therefore unto me by the LORD, that thou wilt not cut off my seed after me, and that thou wilt not destroy my name out of my father's house.²² And David sware unto Saul. And Saul went home; but David and his men gat them up unto the hold.

Saul made an oath to David and David made an oath to Saul not to forget his lineage. Yet, David went back to the stronghold. Hmmmm… David knew he still wasn't to have relationship with

On To The Prize

Saul even though Saul still was anointed of God and was David's father-in-law. He knew Saul's character. David knew God's voice. He knew that he should be wise in dealing with those who practice the works of the flesh.

You are responsible to obey God's Word. You are not responsible for the other person's reactions, actions, thoughts, and/or deeds. They are accountable to God for themselves. No matter what you "do", you cannot make some things right. You can only obey God's Word and pray. It doesn't seem like enough sometimes, but it is. You obeyed God's Word and the Holy Spirit's voice. The other person has to be left in God's hands for recovery, restoration, and discipline. Hear the Holy Spirit's voice and walk on.

It may mean shaking the dust from your feet in some situations. It may mean sitting quietly in the background of the other person's life, being there to help if needed, but not giving of the secrets of your heart. We can't have a "special" relationship with everyone. We are to love no matter what happens. It's not easy to have broken relationships. If you've done what you've known to do according to God's Word, confront, love, and pray, YOU cannot do any more. Leave it in God's hands. David was our example for handling difficult relationships.

Difficult relationships will always be present. Only God can heal them. Your job is to be obedient to the Holy Spirit and God's Word. In the midst of it all God has a plan. He will fulfill His Word:

> **Romans 8:28**
> And we know that all things work together for good to them that love God, to them who are the called according to his purpose.

Let God work it all together for your good.

WARFARE

Judges 3:1-2
1 Now these are the nations which the LORD left, to prove Israel by them, even as many of Israel as had not known all the wars of Canaan; 2 Only that the generations of the children of Israel might know, to teach them war, at the least such as before knew nothing thereof;

There are many Christians who don't believe they have warfare to fight or they refuse to do warfare or haven't had good teaching about the warfare, we, as Christians, encounter. It looks to me by this Scripture in Judges 3 that it's in the plan for all of us to "prove us". God is no respecter of persons. We need to be proved through war. If the Israelites had to do warfare to take their territory, we do too. If they needed to do war to be "proved", to build God's character in them, we need to be proved through war as well. Or, in other words, we need to be in the furnace to be purified.

The interesting thing is that "the generations of children" had to experience it too. No matter how much parents want to protect their children, the generations of children, they have to go through their own warfare for their territory.

You can fight warfare "for" many things in their lives, but you can't fight the warfare "for" their territory. You can fight "with" them just as the children of Israel fought "with" each other to help each tribe claim their territory. Your children still have to do battle to conquer their land, their territory. They have to be transformed into the image of Christ as much as we do. The pressure of tribulation, trials, and warfare transforms us. It is our choice which way we are transformed. We can go "with" God's purpose or "against" God's purpose.

Remember that this Kingdom living is a "together" thing. We are a Body, One Body. If we warfare "together", it is less painful and less work for each person. The job is done quicker, and one person doesn't take the total hit. We must be proved.

> **Timothy 2:21**
> If a man therefore purge himself from these, he shall be a vessel unto honour, sanctified, and meet for the master's use, *and* prepared unto every good work.

Let God "prove" you. Be prepared for every good work.

WISDOM

We've all had the opportunity, much to our own heartbreak at times, to observe God's Word "active" and "inactive" in people's lives. It's very interesting to watch.

Proverbs tells us many times to get KNOWLEDGE and get WISDOM and with all your getting, get UNDERSTANDING.

> **Proverbs 4:7**
> Wisdom *is* the principal thing; *therefore* get wisdom: and with all thy getting get understanding.

> **Proverbs 9:10**
> The fear of the LORD *is* the beginning of wisdom: and the knowledge of the holy *is* understanding.

In the book of James, we are admonished to ask for WISDOM.

> **James 1:5**
> If any of you lack wisdom, let him ask of God, that giveth to all *men* liberally, and upbraideth not; and it shall be given him.

In John's gospel, the Words of Jesus tell us that "apart from Me, you can do nothing".

> **John 15:5**
> I am the vine, ye *are* the branches: He that abideth in me, and I in him, the same bringeth forth much fruit: for without me ye can do nothing.

So, since apart from Him we can do nothing - nothing that will impact His Kingdom, nothing that will make our lives succeed - we NEED to ask for WISDOM in even our everyday tasks and situations. Even when we are doing the familiar and routine, God needs to be in on it. He may have a plan or a change in our comfort zone, our familiar territory.

To live in His Kingdom and do the work of The Kingdom, we have to assume we need all three things in our lives to be effective: KNOWLEDGE, UNDERSTANDING, WISDOM. These are very distinct, different things, yet all work together to bring about the best for us and His Kingdom, for our good and His glory. Just as we are all very distinct, different individuals, we all need to work together to bring about the best for others and for the Kingdom of God on this earth.

I've observed those who have just KNOWLEDGE. They talk about things, yet have no real UNDERSTANDING of what they are talking about. It's all in the HEAD KNOWLEDGE, but they have no HEART KNOWLEDGE. UNDERSTANDING is just that: HEART KNOWLEDGE, the Rhema Word or Revelation.

Then you have people with KNOWLEDGE AND UNDERSTANDING, yet they have no WISDOM in how to use that knowledge and understanding. Because they do have a heart after God and desire to see things work out well for other people, they get in the way of the Holy Spirit many times. The Holy Spirit can't do His job the way God intended because the well-meaning people try to do the work for Him.they have good intentions with poor results. If they had just asked for the WISDOM for the situation before they tried to solve problems or deal with situations, the Holy Spirit would have guided them into ALL TRUTH. So having a lot of knowledge and understanding isn't enough.

Then there are those who have all three: KNOWLEDGE, UNDERSTANDING, and WISDOM. From observation, it appears that the #1 and #2 type people throw a monkey wrench into situations and mess things up. However, #3 type people understand they can't do anything about the "monkey wrenches". The Holy Spirit will do what needs to be done. Number 3 type people know they have to wait on the Lord, be patient, and because they have asked for GOD'S WISDOM, "having done all to stand", they stand and see the salvation of the Lord in the land of the living.

> **Ephesians 6:13**
> Wherefore take unto you the whole armour of God, that ye may be able to withstand in the evil day, and having done all, to stand.

> **2 Chronicles 20:17**
> Ye shall not *need* to fight in this *battle*: set yourselves, stand ye *still*, and see the salvation of the LORD with you, O Judah and Jerusalem: fear not, nor be dismayed; to morrow go out against them: for the LORD *will be* with you.

Just know that God will work things all out for our good because He loves us so much. No matter what other people do to us or say about us or whatever fiery darts the devil throws at us, God is working on our behalf.

You can't help what goes through another person's mind. You can't "work out their salvation with fear and trembling". You can't "tear down their vain imaginations that come against the knowledge of God". You can't "take their thoughts captive". You can't "think on things that are true, noble, just, pure, lovely and of good report" for them. They have to take on those responsibilities. When they don't take on the responsibility for their own lives, they hurt many people around them, yet blame it on other people. In their mind, other people failed them. They don't see where they failed to obey God's Word. If they had been practicing obedience in His Word, so much of what they walk through wouldn't have even taken place. Only the Holy Spirit can reveal that to them.

If you're walking through a similar situation with someone or have observed that with someone in your life, just remember that PRAYER is the most important thing. They will not have "ears to hear" and you can't do anything about that. It is the Holy Spirit Who can do something about it.

Be at peace and remember to ask for WISDOM every day and in every situation.

JONAH

I heard a new twist to the story of Jonah that I'd like to share. It's from the viewpoint of the mariners of the ship. Since then, as I studied the Scripture on the story of Jonah, I have received more revelation and have been able to bring a little more clarity to the whole story as it applies to our lives today.

THE STORY

Jonah hopped on board a boat that was on a mission. They had a destination and the supplies they needed to reach that destination. They already had the plan of action and the cargo they needed to carry out their mission. They were not a passenger boat, but thought they would be kind to Jonah and let him ride along since they assumed they were going the same direction.

When the storm came up, the mariners thought to go back to the shore from which they came to save everyone and everything. It wasn't the direction they were supposed to be going. The storm was too rough no matter what direction they went. Going back to the shore from which they came was not an option.

Jonah told them to throw him overboard. He knew he was running from God. They still wanted to help him. So, they started throwing their supplies and other cargo overboard, things they needed to accomplish their own mission. They thought it would help the situation. Jonah knew he was the cause of it all.

THE POINT

They both were on a mission. They both were valuable to what they were called to do. They shouldn't have been traveling together.

THE REVELATION

Isn't it interesting, the people we let "on board" our lives? We think they are going the same direction. When, in fact, they have a completely different agenda and are along to get a ride to "somewhere" when they are supposed to be going a completely opposite direction. When the raging storms come up, things have to be confronted. Drastic measures have to take place at that point. In "their" storm, we may lose our way and sacrifice our mission. It was a storm we weren't even supposed to be in. Had we kept in step and in time with God's goal and plan of action, we wouldn't have been in someone else's storm at all.

The other question we have to keep in mind is, when we are in the middle of a storm, is it really our storm? We pray all kinds of things when we are in a storm. Examples of prayers we pray are: Oh God, help me! Oh Lord, what have I done? Lord, what do I need to change? What do I need to repent of? Do I need to change directions? What am I doing wrong? AND, all this time we are praying amiss. The Bible says something about praying amiss.

> **James 4:3**
> Ye ask, and receive not, because ye ask amiss, that ye may consume it upon your lusts.

Sometimes we are not praying for the right thing at all.

We have to listen to the Holy Spirit for direction in prayer. It may be the other person we need to be praying for sometimes when the storms are in our lives. It's because of their disobedience to the Father and our zeal and compassion to help someone. But, as the mariners did, sometimes we just take them on board because we think they will benefit us or we will help them. I'm not sure that the mariners had compassion on him because we're not sure the real story he told them to hop on board.

We must remain alert to what the Spirit is saying and where He is leading, so we don't end up in many battles that aren't ours.

Just as in Jonah's story, sometimes God allows the storms to keep us from going back the way we came or from going the wrong direction. Other times we have to be held steady in the middle of things until we can go forward again. Just like the mariners, they couldn't go to either shore until the problem was resolved because of the raging storm.

It's heartbreaking and painful to lose the supplies and cargo needed for our mission, but it's more painful to have to throw our Jonah overboard. Satan likes to throw in distractions that are painfully hard to get out of our lives. But, in the end, it's best for all involved. Jonah is just as valuable in what he's supposed to do, but he causes storms in the lives of others by his disobedience.

Jonah finally obeyed God, but had an attitude problem even after God showed Himself as Savior to him and the people of Nineveh. The mariners weren't the problem. They had nothing to do with the issue of his running from God's call or his attitude. Those were problems Jonah had to work out with God. He made his problems himself. He chose to run from God. He chose to deceive those around him. He stirred up the storms in the mariners lives.

Having said that, here's another bit of advice: Don't be someone else's Jonah.

The mariners were no doubt more careful the next time they decided to let someone on board. They couldn't afford to compromise their mission or risk their lives and the lives of others for the sake of a Jonah.

THE PRACTICAL SIDE

God wants us to be kind and loving, to show mercy and compassion to others. But, sometimes that compassion and mercy is best served by spurring them on to repentance and responsibility. Too many people have an idea of compassion and mercy as "Oh, you poor baby. Let's not let anyone hurt you again". That's not God's mercy and compassion. Mercy isn't stopping pain from happening in someone's life. Mercy is helping them to get on with their mission no matter how painful it may seem. Tell the Truth in love. Support one another in prayer. But, for the sake of all those around and The Kingdom purposes, don't "baby" the children of God. It's time to grow up into Him and take a stand for His Kingdom. Don't be anyone's Jonah and don't allow Jonahs on board.

Get the Jonahs off your boat! That's mercy.

TRUST

I'm sure, since the beginning of time, we have had certain Scriptures backwards in our practice of living a Christian life. There is one practice on which I would like to place my focus. It's the matter of TRUST.

How many times in our lives have we trusted a friend, only to be hurt because they didn't "come through" for us? What we are really saying is that they didn't fulfill our need or want. They didn't meet our expectation. They didn't "prefer" us above themselves or somebody else. They didn't do what we assumed they should do for us or another person. Sounds a little self-absorbed and self-centered.

Because we "trusted" them or had "expectations" of them, we were let down and it affected our relationship. We had to go through all sorts of emotional ups and downs, hurt feelings, separations, healing of emotions, etc. The worst part is that we "judged" them and became critical of them and their walk with God.

The Scripture tells us "not to judge lest we be judged" **(Matthew 7:1)** (Also check **Luke 6**). When we see a brother "overtaken in a fault (or sin)… restore such a one in the spirit of meekness" **(Galatians 6:1).**

Now, the above two Scriptures are very different. If you see someone in a dangerous place, you're not judging. You try to restore. Judging is being critical because they didn't fulfill your expectations of them. I don't see in the Word of God where I'm supposed to expect you to fulfill my desires, needs, or wants.

Proverbs 11:13 implies we are to be "trustworthy": "He who goes about as a talebearer reveals secrets, but he who is trustworthy and faithful in spirit keeps the matter hidden". But, NOWHERE in the Bible does it say to TRUST man. In fact, there are Scriptures that tell us NOT TO TRUST MAN or things made by man (i.e. "don't trust in horses or chariots") or even our own heart.

Jeremiah 9:4
Take ye heed every one of his neighbor, and trust ye not in any brother: for every brother will utterly supplant, and every neighbor will walk with slanders.

Micah 7:5
Trust not in a neighbor; put no confidence in a friend. Keep the doors of your mouth from her who lies in your bosom.

Jeremiah 17:9
The heart is deceitful above all things, and desperately wicked: who can know it?

Now we can't even trust in our own heart!? None of us can say our heart has never tricked us. None of us can say we never had a fleshy desire or an expectation of another. God made us with emotions, but emotions can be handled in the right way or wrong way. He knows we are flesh. He knows the flesh is hard to overcome, but He has made a way of escape. He tells us to crucify the flesh, take our thoughts captive, get wise godly counsel, confess our faults one to another, pray without ceasing, etc. All of these practices keep that deceitful wicked heart in check. When we don't keep it in check, things get out of order in our lives.

Psalm 37:3
Trust in the Lord, and do good; so shalt thou dwell in the land, and verily thou shalt be fed.

There are many Scriptures that tell us to **TRUST GOD**:

Hebrews 2:13; Psalm 18:2; Psalm 18:30; Psalm 31:14; Psalm 4:5; Psalm 37:3-5; Psalm 71:1; Psalm 91:2; Psalm 5:11; Psalm 118:8; Proverbs 3:5; Proverbs 22:19;Isaiah 36:7; Isaiah 50:10 (Not an exhaustive list).

I didn't find a Scripture to tell me to TRUST MAN. But, I did find plenty of Scriptures to tell me to **LOVE MAN**:

1 John 3:14-17; 1 John 4:7-21; Colossians 2:2; 1 Timothy 1:5; Hebrews 13:1;Leviticus 19:18; Proverbs 10:12; Matthew 5:44; John 13:35; John 15:12; Romans 12:9; Romans 13:10; 1 Peter 4:8; 1 Peter 2:17 (Not an exhaustive list).

We, as the Body of Christ, have gotten this backwards. We have tended to TRUST in MAN, and LOVE GOD, when God told us to TRUST GOD and LOVE PEOPLE. Of course, we are to love the Lord our God with all our heart, soul, mind and strength also, but God has made a very strong point in His Word to LOVE people. If we can get that in the right order, there will be a lot less of the works of the flesh operating in the Church.

Let's use the Scripture as a measuring stick, not each other. 1 Corinthians 13 tells us exactly what we need to expect from ourselves as we surrender to Him and let God's love flow through us. If we can't see it, we need more surrender. It's not about "feeling" it. It's about "doing" it. He tells us that "apart from Me, you can do nothing". We can't "do" this on our own. It flows out of relationship with Him.

1 Corinthians 13:4-8
Charity suffereth long, *and* is kind; charity envieth not; charity vaunteth not itself, is not puffed up, Doth not behave itself unseemly, seeketh not her own, is not easily provoked, thinketh no evil; Rejoiceth not in iniquity, but rejoiceth in the truth; Beareth all things, believeth all things, hopeth all things, endureth all things. Charity never faileth: but whether *there be* prophecies, they shall fail; whether *there be* tongues, they shall cease; whether *there be* knowledge, it shall vanish away.

God wants us to love unconditionally as He does. If our emotions get in the way of doing that, then we have put our trust in the flesh.

Remember to TRUST GOD and LOVE MAN.

A CHILD

Watching a child during a long flight can be very entertaining or a big irritation. It was my joy to sit near a well-behaved three year old. He was happy and content. Interaction with his family was loving and his needs and wants were always being attended to by his parents. His mother made sure his needs were met, so he would have a relaxed, comfortable flight.

He never once whined. He just told his mother what he wanted or needed. And she supplied. Drinks, food, entertainment, nap, potty, warmth, love, activity. Many times she anticipated his needs before he even asked.

"Your Father knows what you have need of..."

> **Matthew 6:8**
> Be not ye therefore like unto them: for your Father knoweth what things ye have need of, before ye ask him.

Even when she told him "to wait" or "no" he was good with that. No whining, no pouting, no attitude.

Now, I wish I could say I always reacted to my Heavenly Father like that, but I didn't and I don't. Pouting and whining are a part of many Christians' lives.

I'm thinking this child responded so well because he was taught well. He knew his mother always took care of his needs and wants. He knew discipline. He knew his mother loved him. He knew consequences, I believe.

His mother was kind and gentle with him. She looked at him lovingly and wasn't short with him or aggressive. She had a peaceful demeanor and calmly interacted with him.

His father's behavior toward the child was similar.

So, I'm looking at a very blessed kid. You never saw irritation in the parents' eyes or actions.

So, what's up with us? We don't like to "wait". We don't like "no".

If he got "active" his mother would simply say his name. I wish when I get out of line, all God has to do is say my name.

I'm reaching for that level of trust and response to my Father. I've been practicing it all my life and seem to be better at it…but "blind trust". That's my goal: responding in kindness and love to Him and others.

Just watching this baby's total trust and dependence on his mom and dad was amazing. Watching his independence with buckling and unbuckling his seatbelt, thinking he was doing a great job. Watching him sleep and play. So content.

I want to be content "in whatsoever state" I find myself.

> **Philippians 4:11**
> Not that I speak in respect of want: for I have learned, in whatsoever state I am, therewith to be content.
>
> **1 Timothy 6:6**
> But godliness with contentment is great gain.

Be content with Him.

RELAY RACE

Many changes are happening all around. God is shaking anything that can be shaken in this world and in His Kingdom to separate the goats from the sheep, to get everyone in proper position for the end-time harvest. This is such a great time to be alive.

When I watched the 2012 Summer Olympics, I was reminded of the day in which we live. The relay races were disappointing for the Americans. Both the men's and women's teams dropped the baton in the "TRIALS". Isn't that a real visual for the Kingdom of God?

We each have the baton to carry to finish our course to win the prize. We have taken the baton from the generations before us and have it in hand. And those before us took the baton from the generations before them and passed it on to us. I don't want to drop it in my trials. I don't want to ever drop it. I want to carry it all the way to the end for the prize and finish the race God has set before me.

God has granted us to be alive in such a time as this. Let's keep our grip on what we have to grip, and shake loose what we have to shake loose. Run the race, not looking to the left or right, looking straight ahead, having a forehead like a flint, looking to the Author and Finisher of our faith, keeping our eyes on Him…**our PRIZE**.

Keep your eyes on Him.

LEAH OR RACHAEL?

Revelation 20:12
And I saw the dead, small and great, stand before God; and the books were opened: and another book was opened, which is the book of life: and the dead were judged out of those things which were written in the books, **according to their works**.

Revelation 20:13
And the sea gave up the dead which were in it; and death and hell delivered up the dead which were in them: and they were judged every man **according to their works**.

Revelation 2:3
And I will kill her children with death; and all the churches shall know that I am he which searcheth the reins and hearts: and I will give unto every one of you **according to your works**.

John 15 tells us that God desires that we bear much fruit. AND, He desires that our fruit should remain. The previous verses in Revelation make it clear that we will be judged according to our works that have produced "fruit that remained".

John 15:16
Ye have not chosen me, but I have chosen you, and ordained you, that ye should go and bring forth fruit, and that your fruit should remain: that whatsoever ye shall ask of the Father in my name, he may give it you.

These two different books of the Bible tell me something. They tell me that God wants me to bear fruit for His Kingdom. This also tells me that there is fruit I can produce that will not remain. There will be fruit that will have no value in the Kingdom of God. That's a sobering thought to me.

> **Philippians 4:17**
> Not because I desire a gift: but I desire fruit that may abound to your account.

Abounding in fruit means an **abundance of fruit**. Paul desired that an abundance of fruit would be put on your account. What account? The verses from Revelation tell us that we are rewarded and judged according to our works. We have an account in Heaven.

> **Titus 3:14**
> And let us also learn to maintain good works for necessary uses, that they be not unfruitful.

This verse tells me to maintain good works and that my works be not unfruitful. I believe God is trying to make a point to us. He has placed the discussion of "fruit" and "works" all over the New Testament teachings.

> **James 2:26**
> For as the body without the spirit is dead, so faith without works is dead also.

It appears to be about our level of faith. We will do good works and bear fruit because of the faith we have in our Savior.

> **1 Peter 2:12**
> Having your conversation honest among the Gentiles: that, whereas they speak against you as evildoers, they may by your good works, which they shall behold, glorify God in the day of visitation.

There also are different reasons to bear fruit. Your works will bring some to glorify God and build the Kingdom of God, thereby, bringing lasting fruit.

Works are so important to God that He wants us to provoke each other to do good works.

> **Hebrews 10:24**
> And let us consider one another to provoke unto love and to good works.

Not only do we provoke one another to good works, but we need to be careful to maintain good works. We are to be constantly maintaining the good works and not get weary in well-doing (Galatians 6:9; 2 Thessalonians 3:13). We are always to be looking out for the other person's best interest and preferring another above ourselves (1 Timothy 5:21; Romans 12:10). The Word tells us these are good and profitable to men.

> **Titus 3:8**
> This is a faithful saying, and these things I will that thou affirm constantly, that they which have believed in God might be careful to maintain good works. These things are good and profitable unto men.

The other interesting thing I found out about the importance of bearing fruit is in the Old Testament.

> **Hosea 10:1**
> Israel is an empty vine, he bringeth forth fruit unto himself: **according to the multitude of his fruit he hath increased the altars;** according to the goodness of his land they have made goodly images.

The point of this Scripture lies in **the multitude of fruit**. What does it do? It increases the altar. What is an altar? A place of repentance, sacrifice, humility and redemption. Why is that increase a good thing? It increases our godly character. The larger the altar, the more visible it is. The more visible, the more it reminds us to repent, to humble ourselves, to sacrifice. The more that happens, the more godly character we develop. The more godly character we develop, the more impact we can make on those around us, thereby, increasing the Kingdom of God.

The more visible our altar, or our good works and our godly character, the more people will see the goodness of God in the land of the living and see God's goodness through our works and repent.

> **Psalm 116:9**
> I will walk before the LORD in the land of the living.

> **Psalm 27:13**
> I had fainted, unless I had believed to see the goodness of the LORD in the land of the living.

> **Matthew 5:16**
> Let your light so shine before men, that they may see your good works, and glorify your Father which is in heaven.

No matter what's going on in our lives, we should be thinking about "bringing forth fruit unto God". Our goal should be to "bear much fruit". Our focus should be on building the Kingdom of God.

> **Matthew 6:20**
> But **lay up for yourselves treasures in heaven**, where neither moth nor rust doth corrupt, and where thieves do not break through nor steal;

> **Luke 12:34**
> For where **your treasure** is, there will your heart be also.

God tells us to lay up treasures in Heaven. What is your treasure? Ministry? Gifts? Talents? Earthly possessions? People? Acceptance? Dreams? Visions? Expectations? Accomplishments?
Have we multiplied our treasures into the Kingdom of God? Have we born much fruit? Have we born fruit that will remain? Are we

satisfied with "some fruit" and "more fruit", when God wants us to have "much fruit"?

Only God knows what is best for us. Only God knows what will cause us to lay up more treasures in Heaven. Only God sees the whole picture. This brings us to the main story of this chapter: Leah or Rachael.

Chapters 29-46 of Genesis tell the story of Jacob going after the wife he wanted. I will just give a few excerpts from those Scriptures to make some very important points for our Christian walk today.

> **Genesis 29:16-17**
> And Laban had two daughters: the name of the elder was Leah, and the name of the younger was Rachel. Leah was tender-eyed; but Rachel was beautiful and well favoured.
>
> **Genesis 30:1-4**
> And when Rachel saw that she bare Jacob no children, Rachel envied her sister; and said unto Jacob, Give me children, or else I die. And Jacob's anger was kindled against Rachel: and he said, Am I in God's stead, who hath withheld from thee the fruit of the womb? And she said, Behold my maid Bilhah, go in unto her; and she shall bear upon my knees, that I may also have children by her. And she gave him Bilhah her handmaid to wife: and Jacob went in unto her And Bilhah conceived, and bare Jacob a son.
>
> **Genesis 30:20**
> And Leah said, God hath endued me with a good dowry; now will my husband dwell with me, because I have born him six sons:

The Story

Leah was the one that didn't look so good. She was so much harder for Jacob to love. She was not the object of Jacob's affection. Through a little research I found out that her "tender-eyed" description could mean a few different things: She didn't have pretty eyes, was cross-eyed, or was always crying so her eyes looked dull and puffy most of the time. But the ultimate thing is that she wasn't attractive to Jacob.

Rachel was the beautiful one… the one he loved… the one Jacob wanted.

Both Rachael and Leah helped build the Kingdom of Israel.

Leah was the one that would be more fruitful and was given the place of most honor in the family. She was buried with the Patriarchs.

Rachel died first.

Application

Leah represents what the Father wants to give us. There may be things we feel called to do, but it isn't as attractive to us as something else. It could be something that looks too hard for us, or too complicated, or something that may tend to overwhelm us. It could be a type or place of ministry that doesn't seem as good or as rewarding to us, or we don't feel we fit together with well. There may be something we believe we are called to do that seems so hard because of relationships. The circumstances in certain situations aren't what we expected. Sometimes we say to ourselves, "After all, I've served God for so many years, surely things should start to go much smoother and be beautiful and more…."

Rachel represents what we want. She represents how we envision ourselves and our lives. She is the way we think our lives should be. She represents places we think we should be or the way we think our ministry should look like, the way we think our lives should look, after all these years of serving God, we should know… right?

Sometimes we have our eyes on the wrong things about ministry. Sometimes our eyes are not on the right things as we live our everyday lives. We have our heart and mind on what pleases us, what we think will bring happiness, fruit, joy, peace. But, God is the one who knows what will produce the most lasting and abundant fruit in our lives.

The one situation has your heart but is less fruitful Your Rachael. God knows that what you may strive for, or the fruit you would produce by having what you wanted would not be given high honor in the end: the honor of glorifying God forever.

Leah, what the Father wants to give you, would bring the highest honor in the end by giving the most glory to God. Leah would produce abundant and lasting fruit that builds the Kingdom of Heaven.

It doesn't mean you can't enjoy what God has placed in your life or called you to do. Leah is a loveable woman. She just isn't what you wanted. You could still enjoy, but have to change the attitude of your mind and heart to grasp God's wisdom in your circumstances.

So we have a choice, more fruit or much fruit. Both Leah and Rachael had "fruit that remained". Leah had "much fruit".

I want Leah; what the Father wants to give me.

Ultimately, God wants Leah and Rachel to be one and the same. So we have both; what He wants to give us and what we love.

> **Hebrews 12:1-2**
> Wherefore seeing we also are compassed about with so great a cloud of witnesses, let us lay aside every weight, and the sin which doth so easily beset us, and let us run with patience the race that is set before us, looking unto Jesus the author and finisher of our faith; who for the joy that was set before him endured the cross, despising the shame, and is set down at the right hand of the throne of God.

1 Corinthians 9:2
Know ye not that they which run in a race run all, but one receiveth the prize? So run, that ye may obtain.

Take your Leah. He will give you your Rachel.

About the Author

Renee Hibma was born and raised in Holland, Michigan. She went to Trinity Bible Institute (now College) in Ellendale, North Dakota where she earned her Bachelor of Arts (BA) degree in Bible General with a minor in Missions. During her four years at Trinity, she traveled with the Trinity Troubadours singing all over the United States every summer. The leaders, Bob and Kaye Garrison, were careful to teach the Troubadours how to hear the voice of the Holy Spirit and learn how to operate in the gifts of the Spirit while ministering to others.

After Trinity, Renee attended the Assemblies of God Graduate School (now Theological Seminary) in Springfield, Missouri where she graduated with a Master of Arts (MA) degree in Cross-Cultural Communications. She attended nursing school at the University of Tennessee in Memphis, Tennessee, and received two degrees: Bachelor of Science in Nursing (BSN) and Master of Science in Nursing (MSN). In 2006, Renee finished her Doctorate of Ministry (D.Min.) degree in Biblical Counseling at Trinity College of the Bible and Seminary in Newburgh, Indiana.

Renee has been the worship leader, or as she prefers to call it, the "lead worshiper", at three different churches over the last several years. She has been singing, guest speaking, teaching women's Bible studies and Sunday School for almost four decades. Renee has been an ordained minister since 1999 with Evangel Fellowship International (EFI). She has been officially doing counseling since 2002. Renee started working as a Family Nurse Practitioner (FNP-BC) in rural health centers in 1995.

She is officially a "snowbird" now and splits her time between Michigan and Florida.

God has given her a gift to write about what she believes will encourage others in their walk with God. Her hope is that through the pages of her books the readers will find encouragement, comfort, strength, hope, and healing.

Contact her at: revdrrenee@juno.com.
Read her blog at: reneehibma.blogspot.com